DAUNTLESS
in Mississippi

THE LIFE OF SARAH A. DICKEY

1838 – 1904

by Helen Griffith

DAUNTLESS IN MISSISSIPPI

SARAH A. DICKEY

DAUNTLESS
in Mississippi

THE LIFE OF SARAH A. DICKEY
1838 – 1904

by Helen Griffith

DINOSAUR PRESS

To E.C.J.

Foreword

MY INTRODUCTION to Sarah A. Dickey was in Mississippi at Tougaloo College. In the entrance hall of the Sarah A. Dickey Memorial Hospital was a large portrait of a commanding, Victorian-looking woman beneath which hung a framed diploma stating that Sarah A. Dickey had graduated from Mount Holyoke Seminary in 1869. My curiosity was aroused. During my thirty-five years of teaching at Mount Holyoke College, I had never heard her name. As a guest teacher at Tougaloo I had opportunity to put my question to everyone from the president on. No one knew who Sarah Dickey was. Perhaps she was the first nurse, the registrar surmised.

What I found out about her the following summer in the carefully kept Mount Holyoke Alumnae archives raised my interest to the boiling point and led me, on my return to Tougaloo that fall, to spend my spare time in the nearby town of Clinton. For Clinton was where Mount Hermon Seminary, the school Sarah Dickey founded, once stood. Except for her grave on the former Mount Hermon campus and a big brass bell at the public school there, I found no material reminders of her more than thirty years in the town. But when I sought people who might have known her, I struck a rich vein. There were still Negroes living in and around Clinton who had gone to Mount Hermon or worked on the grounds. Their memories of Sarah Dickey were warm and vivid. They directed me to others living farther afield who had known her.

A third source of information came from the generous cooperation of two successive curators of the Historical Society of the Evangelical United Brethren Church, Dr. Arthur Core and Rev. John Ness, Jr. Their spirit — as well as hers — is suggested by this remark in a letter from Mr. Ness: "Whenever I need an uplift in spirit, I start looking for more Sarah Dickey references. Her dedication buoys me up." Eight years before Sarah Dickey's death in 1904 she became an ordained minister in the Evangelical United Brethren Church, a fact either unknown or unremembered among my Mississippi informants and unrecorded in the Mount Holyoke material.

Sarah Dickey's life is the story of a Northern white woman in the second half of the nineteenth century, a woman dauntless in the face of almost insuperable obstacles. She possessed great courage and complete faith. Her experience teaching the just emancipated slaves in Vicksburg during the last nineteen months of the war made her decide to devote her life to the education of the freedmen. Her experience at Mount Holyoke Seminary where she worked her way through the four-year course determined the form that work was to take. She would found a school on the plan of Mount Holyoke for young colored women in Mississippi. Though she had neither money nor influence, she did just that. She returned to Mississippi the year the Reconstruction government was installed and taught in one of the first Negro public schools. There she courageously withstood repeated attempts of the Ku Klux Klan to drive her away, making it quite clear that only death could remove her. In 1875, the year the Reconstruction government was overthrown, she opened her own school, Mount Hermon Seminary. For the remaining twenty-nine years of her life she was not only principal of the growing institution, but singlehanded raised most of the funds needed for maintenance, salaries, repairs and buildings. Students prepared at Mount Hermon were in considerable demand. During the lifetime of the school she was fittingly called the Mary Lyon of the South.

Sarah Dickey's life is also a story of the growth of friendly race relations in a town where she was at first completely ostracized, a town in which one of the worst race riots occurred the very year her school opened. Yet long before her death her bravery, tact and patience in meeting and disarming opposition had won for her and her school an honored place in the community. In short, this is the story of a life that commands attention today and makes us proud to belong to the human race.

HELEN GRIFFITH

South Hadley, Massachusetts

May, 1965

Acknowledgments

THIS LIFE OF Sarah A. Dickey was begun long ago. The project was twice abandoned, once for lack of biographical material (I still know almost nothing about Sarah Dickey's family and ancestry) and once, after I returned North, because of competing interests. At the time I began the work I made connections with those who had been students at Mount Hermon in Sarah Dickey's day or who had known her in other ways. I took full notes on what they told me, which fortunately I kept. Two of this group became my personal friends, Mr. and Mrs. Claude Inge. Whenever I went to see them in their attractive Jackson home, we talked about their dear Miss Dickey. They fed my interest in that remarkable woman. Mr. Inge had been brought up by her from the time he was eight years old. His wife, Mrs. Alice Wells Inge, one of five daughters their well-to-do father had sent to Mount Hermon Seminary, had graduated from it in 1904. I am deeply indebted to both of them for their reminiscences.

I would like also to thank and record the names of others whose memories of Miss Dickey I have used: Mr. Allen Putnam (a special debt to him for the Mount Hermon catalogues he had saved), Mrs. Mary Caldwell Coats, Miss Addie Wells, Mrs. Lizella Bradley Harris, Mrs. Nannie Williams O'Neill, Mrs. Elvira Williams Arrington, Mrs. Pinkie Bracey Williams, Mr. Paul Walker, Mrs. Abi Holly, Mrs. Agnes Johnson Poole, Mr. Tom Dawson and Mrs. Ellen Butler, whose granddaughter took me to Sarah Dickey's grave. The above all lived either in the Clinton or the Jackson area. I traveled farther to interview Mrs. Stella Moulton High at Canton, Mrs. L. T. Miller at Yazoo City and Mrs. Willette Campbell Davis at Little Rock, Arkansas.

There were also a few white residents in Clinton and Jackson from whom I got some information and verification — the Misses Timberlake, and others. Though I was able to track down and interview briefly Mrs. Ruth Fox Cone, who had taught at Mount Hermon three years before Sarah Dickey's death and continued to teach there until the school was given up, I lost her almost immediately. She had gone from the Chicago apartment where I had found her, leaving no forwarding address behind. But at least I had the satisfaction of seeing her and hearing her account of Sarah Dickey's last words, and for that I am grateful. Other firsthand information came from a Mount Holyoke graduate whom I had known a long time, but had not known until recently that she had taught at Tougaloo College during the last days of Mount Hermon Seminary. She was able to fill in some gaps that had troubled me. I am thankful the material came in time to be used and very grateful to Dr. Lillian Voorhees, Professor Emeritus of Fisk University, for putting aside her work to help me.

When it comes to debts of gratitude to libraries and librarians, I have a goodly number to acknowledge. First comes the Mount Holyoke College library where needed help in using the rich material in the college archives was given me first by Miss Bertha E. Blakely, librarian emeritus, and later by Miss Flora Belle Ludington, librarian, and her administrative assistant, Mrs. Virginia Spencer. The library was helpful in other ways. Interlibrary loans made it possible for me to consult at Mount Holyoke the Yale Library volumes of the Proceedings of the Trustees of the John F. Slater Fund for the Education of Freedmen and from the Hampshire Inter-Library Center at the University of Massachusetts, catalogues of those colleges for men in the 1860's used for comparison with what was educationally available to women at that time.

American Missionary Association material I had tried earlier to consult at Fisk is now classified and in the competent care of Fisk's reference librarian, Mrs. Virginia Potts, who located some of the material I wanted and had Xerox copies made of it for me. I send her my thanks. Indeed I would extend thanks to all those librarians, not a few, who imaginatively shared my problems and found material unknown to me. Such a one has already been mentioned, Rev. John Ness, Jr., curator of the Dayton depository for the Historical Society of the Evangelical United Brethren Church. He is the one responsible for my return to writing this biography. For by indicating a use to which he hoped to put it, he made its completion seem worth while. His research in scattered and little known church papers and in minutes of board and committee meetings inaccessible to me, the time and interest he gave the search and the considerable material he unearthed make anything I can say by way of thanks inadequate.

My gratitude goes also to the curator of the Brown University alumni records kept in the John Hay Library, that rich treasure house of Americana. He produced a fat folder devoted entirely to Sarah Dickey's friend and trustee, Walter Hillman of the class of 1854. Before I close this list of friendly institutions I must gratefully mention the courteous attention I received at the public buildings in Jackson and Raymond where I went to consult various documents.

One group to which many writers are much indebted is that of their personal friends. Here I have been uncommonly blessed. I can truthfully say in the words of the conventional formula that without their interest and encouragement this biography might never have been written. Some of them gave much more than interest and encouragement, for they were editors or writers themselves. Two offered to read the finished manuscript and did so. Two other friends were drafted, a captive audience, to listen to my reading much of it aloud; others had to listen to separate chapters when we were on summer holiday, and one worked on two chapters in an effort to instruct me in editorial practices. They all made useful suggestions along their various lines. Even the one who regularly fell asleep as I read of a summer evening provided criticism by that very act. Perhaps the most useful criticism was that which turned me from a fictional approach which I knew in my heart of hearts to be wrong but had fallen into because it was so much more fun to do. I feel warmly grateful to each and all and herewith inscribe their names Quaker fashion without their fine handles: Emily Cooper Johnson, Edith Longstreth Wood, Miriam Mulford Thrall, Lois Comings Bertholf, Sydney Robertson McLean, Ruth Eldred Fairbank, Mary Taggart Dillon, and Olga W. Vickery. The above are listed according to the length of my friendship with them; the top two have been my friends for sixty-three years, the last for only twelve. They are a patient, hardy lot, enduring me and my enthusiasms without too much complaint. I did not expect any new friend I might acquire to have such hardihood. But one has appeared and out of a clear sky volunteered to find a printer for Sarah Dickey, edit the manuscript and see it through the press. The day of miracles has not gone by. I do not know how to thank her.

There is another group of my friends who do not know they are contributing to the life of Sarah Dickey. They are former students who made up a generous purse as a gift on my eightieth birthday. When I thanked them I had not decided how I would use the money. Now that it goes into helping Sarah Dickey come to life I want to thank them again.

Because they are paid for their work, typists (unless they are devoted wives of Ph.D. aspirants) seldom receive mention. I enjoyed working with mine and want to thank them. They have shown skill in deciphering my interlinings and sometimes cryptic instructions. Miss Martha Bates typed most of the first draft. A few chapters were done by a Mount Holyoke undergraduate, Miss Kathryn Genovese. At another time Mrs. Helen Freeman Vannett, assistant in the art department at

Mount Holyoke, devoted most of her scanty free time to keeping up with my frequent revisions. The handsome final draft was typed by a Mount Holyoke alumna living in South Hadley, Mrs. Constance Italia Bagg. The interest of each in Sarah Dickey was heartening.

There is still a last indebtedness that I had expected to acknowledge by letter, but the death last year of Dr. Vernon Lane Wharton, author of *The Negro in Mississippi, 1865-1890,* makes a personal thank-you impossible. His scholarly monograph, so rich in well-documented detail, stands out from the many books I read for the Mississippi background. Dr. Wharton was teaching at Millsaps College in Jackson during part of the time I was at Tougaloo and came out several times a week to give a course there. Mississippi was his native state, and Millsaps, his college. He told me that when he went to the University of North Carolina to work for his doctorate, he had no particular interest in the Negro and felt about him as most average white young Mississippians did. He chose his subject, he said, simply because he thought it would give him a better chance at scholarship aid, for the Rosenwald money had just been made available for work on and for the Negro. What his thorough research uncovered completely overturned all his previously held ideas about the treatment of the Negro in the South. He was greatly concerned lest the changes already in the air should find the Negro unprepared for the responsibilities ahead. He constantly urged the students at Tougaloo to take their college work more seriously. Because these conversations with Dr. Wharton focused my interest and colored my thinking and because his monograph furnished me with so much factual material, I tender this posthumous note of thanks.

Contents

1.   Now Is The Time

THE YEAR was 1872, only two years after Mississippi had reluctantly accepted Negro suffrage as part of the price for being readmitted to the Union. The place was the home of a Negro state senator in Clinton, a town some ten miles west of Jackson, the state capital. Boarding with Senator Charles Caldwell and his wife was Sarah Ann Dickey, an 1869 graduate of Mount Holyoke Seminary and at the moment in charge of one of the first Negro public schools set up by the hated post-war Reconstruction government for the freedmen in Mississippi. When no white family would take Sarah Dickey in, the Caldwells had offered her a place to live, an offer she was glad to accept. Charles Caldwell had bought a large, comfortable house in town when it came on the market after the war, as so many houses did. An intelligent, self-educated Negro, he had considerable influence among the colored people of the state, though the white residents of Clinton probably thought of him as the one-time slave who had shoed their horses. Sarah Dickey had come to respect his judgment and profited by talking over her school problems with him. She had even confided to him her purpose in coming to Mississippi.

On the particular late December day of which I write — it was during the Christmas recess — she was sitting in her room sewing when she had an experience that determined the future course of her life and, through her, influenced hundreds of other lives. In an account of it written years later she says,

. . . suddenly there seemed to come before me a flash of light, and a voice said "Now is the time to begin your work." I laid down my sewing and at once made the necessary preparation to go to Jackson the

1

next day and lay my plans before the friends I had already selected in my mind for trustees. Without a dollar on hand at the time I thank our dear Lord that "I was not disobedient to the heavenly vision," but went straight forward and the result is Mt. Hermon Seminary at Clinton, Mississippi.

That it was a heavenly vision she did not doubt, nor was it her first. For years she had lived under a strong sense of divine guidance. Under it she had joined the United Brethren Mission in Vicksburg to teach the just emancipated Negroes, who were pouring into the town during the last two years of the war. Under divine guidance she had dedicated herself to their education. At the close of the war, when she felt the need to prepare herself more fully for the work she was to undertake, the same guiding voice led her to Mount Holyoke Seminary. She tells us that once, briefly, she had questioned its source. That was when, near the beginning of her difficult four-year course, the familiar voice (the adjective is hers) told her that she must build a school like Mount Holyoke for Negro girls in Mississippi. The thought of such an undertaking overwhelmed her. She knew she lacked everything needed for it — money, friends, influence, knowledge and experience. Though ways and means were hidden from her, the strong sense that she was under divine guidance gave her strength for the grueling work of those years of preparation and focused her efforts. The idea of her future work became part of her life.

So when she heard "Now is the time to begin your life work," the meaning was clear to her — the time to take those preliminary steps necessary for the work entrusted to her, that of founding a Mount Holyoke for Negro girls. She had thought about it so long that now she knew exactly what she must do. Like Mount Holyoke, her school must have a Board of Trustees, and she wanted both white and colored men on it. In Jackson were various people with whom she had connections, some of them from her Vicksburg days, others from her more recent past. She had already been in the state for two years, first at a mission school in Raymond, county seat of Hinds County, then, during the summer, in social work for Negroes in the country around Raymond, and finally at Clinton in her present position. Everywhere she had made friends and picked up ideas. She no longer felt overwhelmed. "Now is the time" came as a welcome command.

In a way her whole life had been shaping her for this work. The passionate desires of her bleak and thwarted girlhood played an important part. Her mother had died when she was only eight. Speaking later of this loss, she said that all through her life she had had a very real sense of her mother's tender presence, almost like that of a guardian angel. It may very well be that this sense is what kept her from being resentful or bitter at the way she was treated after her mother's death. In telling about her hard experiences she protected her relatives by never mentioning any of their names and by never passing judgment.

For her father, ineffectual man as he seems to have been, she always felt warm affection. In her will written a few days before her death in 1904, she mentions "some books and souvenirs given me by my father."

At the time of her mother's death in 1846, her father, a poor man, had no alternative but to parcel out at least some of his eight children among relatives. Some of the relatives were living in what was then a sparsely settled farming section of southwestern Ohio. Sarah was given to an aunt who promised that the child, in return for helping about the place, should go to school. A sturdy little girl can be very useful in pioneering country. It may be that Sarah, driven in on herself by this break in her life, seemed to her busy aunt stolid, not very bright, not likely to benefit from schooling. Also her aunt lived in an isolated section with no school conveniently near. Meanwhile, her father apparently had gone away, perhaps seeking work elsewhere. At all events, when he returned at the time of her aunt's death, nearly five years later, he found that his thirteen-year-old daughter had not had one day of schooling and could neither read nor write. Her religious life had been equally neglected. That Sarah herself suffered keenly from these deprivations we know from what she said later, although she never spoke harshly of those who had made a household drudge of her. But she must have confided to her father her burning desire for schooling.

He placed her with a widow who had been left with a farm to manage on the understanding that Sarah must go to school. And she did — for nearly four weeks. Then she broke down from the hard physical labor and exposure to all kinds of weather. Among her farm duties, she had been responsible for driving the cows a rugged mile to pasture every morning and back again in the afternoon as soon as school was out. This experience probably laid the foundation for her rheumatic troubles in later years.

When she recovered, her father arranged to have some cousins take her, again on the understanding that she be allowed to attend school. The bargain was poorly kept. In the two years she was with them she got to school not more than ten to fifteen days each winter. So at sixteen, though she could read and spell a little, she could not write. What she learned, however, had been enough to give form to the stirrings within her. She announced that she wanted to be a teacher. Her relatives and friends took the idea as a huge joke. (She was evidently not regarded as very capable.) But when they found that she was serious, they tried to explain why such a career would be out of the question for her. They told her it was too late to harbor such a notion, for she was way behind her age in school. Even if she weren't, she could not afford the time and money it would take to prepare herself. And finally when they found her unconvinced, they flatly declared that she lacked the capacity to make a good teacher. They advised her to choose something within her reach. She did not argue the point, but she could not silence something within her that made her look at this matter and many other things in a different way from those about her.

Take the question of slavery, for instance. Though Ohio was not a slave-holding state, the section in which she lived was largely pro-slavery at that time. Yet everything she heard about the system as she grew up and especially the cruelty, as it seemed to her, of depriving children of school privileges just

because of their color, aroused her compassion. She knew at
first hand the torment of such deprivation.

And in a matter so close to her as her own future, she followed not the thinking of her elders but the promptings of the
inward guide that was to direct her throughout her life. If her
relatives did not believe that she would profit by more education, they would have no interest in helping her to get more.
She must take matters into her own hands. And she did.

She found a family that she describes only as "kind neighbors." She struck a bargain with them. For her room and board
she would work for them in the morning before she left for
school and again in the afternoon and evening after school
was over. At long last she had an opportunity to attend school
regularly. That most of the pupils were children, while she was
already sixteen when she began, mattered not one bit. Her
great hunger was being assuaged; the goal she had set herself
of becoming a teacher glimmered on the horizon.

To the astonishment of her relatives, at the end of three years
of this intensive work, she applied for and received a teacher's
certificate. When one remembers that at thirteen she could
neither read nor write, that at sixteen she could read a little
but not write, and now at nineteen, after only three years of
consecutive schooling, she had won a certificate to teach, one
realizes something of the passion of her desire, the quality of
her mind, and her extraordinary capacity for hard work.

The nameless "kind neighbor's" household numbered fourteen. She got up at four o'clock every morning and worked for
the family till school time and then, returning at four o'clock
in the afternoon, she worked till the family's ten o'clock bedtime, sewing for them as well as doing household chores. After
the family had gone to bed, she turned to her own affairs —
preparing her lessons, washing and mending her clothes,
making them, too. She speaks of two calico dresses for school
and a gingham one for Sunday.

Under such a regime she would have foundered had she not
been upheld by her passionate desire, now powerfully reinforced by a new element that came into her life at this time.

giving greater meaning as well as form and focus to that desire. She has told us that although she had had no religious instruction, she had always felt a reaching out of her spirit and a sense of being guided by something that was both within and beyond her. Now she came under the influence of the Church of the United Brethren in Christ, as the Evangelical United Brethren Church was then called. On her twentieth birthday, April 25, 1858, she became a member of that church, a relationship that meant much to her all through her life. Indeed, at the time of her death many years later, she had been an ordained United Brethren minister for eight years, although in Mississippi she seems to have made little use of the position.

The year of 1857-58 was important to her in another way, for in the fall of '57 she began teaching. Her first school was in Lewisburg, a town some twenty miles northwest of Dayton and nine miles from where she was living, a daily walk for her of eighteen miles. The school itself had the reputation of being hard to manage, but to the surprise of everyone and especially of her relatives, she was notably successful. From then on she had no difficulty finding places to teach. But since her hungry mind still craved further education, she spent the next few years alternating between teaching and study. Her childhood idea of helping slave children to read was obviously out of the question. Laws in all the Southern states prohibited teaching slaves to read and write. Moreover, the country was in ferment, on the edge of civil war. So she turned to the idea of foreign missions. The United Brethren had a mission in Sierra Leone, West Africa. She talked the matter over with some members of the Mission Board and applied for an appointment there. The grief she felt on not being accepted shows how much she had counted on the appointment. After her death some forty-seven years later the money she had willed to the United Brethren's Board of Missions was appropriately applied to that same Sierra Leone Mission.

The strength of Sarah Dickey's expectation had been partly due to a dream she had had, a dream that recurred from time to time in these years. In her dream she found herself walking in a deep, dark wood. At first she did not know which way to turn, for there was no path. But after a little, uncertainty left her; she felt directed. Following this leading she at last came to the edge of the wood. A great meadow lay below her, but a wall kept her from entering it. She sought an opening in vain. Her distress at her failure would always waken her. She needed no Joseph to interpret. She was sure that the meadow represented the field of work to which God had called her. The wall kept her out of it. At first she identified the field with mission work in Africa and the wall with whatever had kept her from being appointed. But as the dream continued to recur, she looked for other significance.

Except for Lewisburg we do not know where she taught or where she studied in the years that followed. We do know, however, that she secured a good secondary-school education somewhere, for later she was able to pass the entrance examinations for Mount Holyoke Seminary. She told of joining the church, of her dream and of her disappointment about the African mission, but other than those three matters she never mentioned these years. Yet they must have been rich years for her — the study and teaching, the church life, the new friends, the widening experiences. Since they were momentous years for the country, perhaps it is not strange that the ordinary details of country school teaching and classroom study were swallowed up by what was happening about her.

Her lifelong interest in public affairs probably started at this time. An ardent Republican, she would have rejoiced at Abraham Lincoln's election as President in November, 1860. But when, even before his inauguration, South Carolina, followed by six other states, seceded from the Union and formed the Confederate States of America, she must have realized to what a pass the country had come. In the next month, on April 12, the first shot was fired in that bloody and hotly contested war which was to last four dreadful years.

During its course, however, one cheering thing happened, something that affected Sarah Dickey's life and determined its later direction. That something was the Emancipation Proclamation which became effective on the first day of January, 1863. The Proclamation spurred the Mission Board of the United Brethren Church to immediate action. The church had long suffered from its locally unpopular antislavery stand. As the report of a May 1863 meeting of its Mission Board put it, "Our anti-slavery Discipline is now rather in our favor, instead of against us, as formerly. . . ." The Mission Board forthwith started on plans for establishing a center somewhere in the lower Mississippi states to serve the just emancipated slaves as well as any "destitute whites with whom we may come in contact." Money was appropriated and a general appeal for funds made. The Mission was to have a double purpose: to provide "books and instruction for the mind" as well as "the gospel of Christ for the soul."

Money poured in, exceeding the Board's most sanguine expectations, and plans took shape. Rev. B. F. Morgan and Rev. William McKee were commissioned to find a suitable site and make necessary preparations. They left in early September. While they were gone three teachers for the Mission were chosen: Ettie G. Stubbs of Butler County, Ohio; Minnie E. Hanson of Shiremanstown, Pennsylvania; and Sarah A. Dickey of Dayton, Ohio. How eagerly they must have awaited word from the reconnoiterers! At last it came. Vicksburg had been chosen, a city which two months before, on July 4, 1863 had finally surrendered to General Grant after a six weeks' siege and a preceding eight months of general skirmishing. Its possession gave Union forces almost complete command of the Mississippi River. The emissaries reported that they had secured the use of a large abandoned church. It would serve as school on weekdays and church on Sundays. As soon as the work was started Mr. Morgan would return North to get his wife, the three young lady teachers, and needed supplies. Mr. McKee would carry on both school and church in his absence and afterward go farther south to establish a second mission at Davis Bend.

This plan was carried out. When Mr. Morgan returned North he was able to report that they had started the school on October 19, 1863 and that by the time he left, a week later, three hundred pupils had enrolled, each paying a registration fee of fifteen cents. Plenty of work for three teachers!

Unfortunately we have no firsthand account of Sarah Dickey's river boat journey to Vicksburg. Probably the party took the boat at Cincinnati and steamed down the Ohio, stopping at Louisville, Paducah, and Cairo, where the great Ohio River joins the greater Mississippi. The trip as far as Memphis, if not easy, was not dangerous. But from Memphis on down, there was real danger, for fighting was still going on in the hostile states that flanked the river. On the Mississippi side Confederate General Forrest was skilfully deploying his troops for guerrilla attacks. The travelers knew that some Presbyterian missionaries who had preceded them had been fired at from the shore and one of their number killed; there were anxious hours before the party finally landed at Vicksburg on December 11, 1863.

The war-scarred city presented a strange sight to the eyes of these travelers. It was not so much the shell-riddled buildings that appalled, though there was scarcely a building left standing that did not bear marks of the recent fighting; it was rather the teeming life that poured through the narrow, steep streets. One wonders, did Sarah Dickey have a premonition that among these people or others like them her life was to be lived? It is certain that none of the newcomers had ever before seen so many dark faces. Negro fugitives had been inundating Vicksburg since its occupation by Union troops; sometimes as many as a thousand came in a single day. It has been estimated that there may have been about thirty thousand Negroes in and about Vicksburg at this time. Some walked proudly in Union uniforms. Sarah Dickey told with a twinkle in her eye of the soldier who had confided to her that he had joined the army "for the ornamental of it." The decision to use Negro soldiers had been made earlier in '63, and because so many Union soldiers objected to having them in their companies, they were organized separately under white officers. A regiment of colored troops was stationed in Vicksburg.

But except for the soldiers and a few others, those the new-comers saw as they were driven from the boat landing to the building where they were to live must have stirred their pity. There seemed to be hordes of Negroes everywhere, living under the worst possible slum conditions of overcrowding and filth. Yet miserably ragged and battered as these Negroes appeared, there was something eager and hopeful about the way they eyed this wagon-load of northern "white folks" with their furniture who had come down the river to help them.

The building before which the party finally stopped was out-side the fortifications. During the siege it had been used by the Union army as a hospital. On the first floor was the office of Col. Samuel Thomas, superintendent of the "contrabands," the name given to the Negroes who had fled from their former masters to the protection of the Union army — a curious and, certainly after the Emancipation Proclamation, an inaccurate term for them, implying, as it does, that they were property. Dr. Joseph Warren probably also had an office in the building. He was chaplain of the Negro regiment; Sarah Dickey later worked with him on Negro marriages. Samuel Thomas and Joseph Warren were the two men charged with the care of the Negroes thronging Vicksburg. Fortunately they both had re-spect for and belief in these refugees, in sharp contrast to some of those in command who saw in them only a burden on the army.

Burden they certainly were. From the beginning of the war, fugitive slaves constituted a big problem for the army. At first each general handled those within his lines as he saw fit, some even returning them to their owners. But as their numbers grew and the discrepancies in treatment became more apparent, it was clear that there must be a central policy and a plan to imple-ment it. So in November, 1862 General Grant appointed one of his chaplains, John Eaton, to undertake what was, under the circumstances, an almost impossible task. The choice could hardly have been better, for John Eaton, a Dartmouth graduate in his early thirties, possessed both vision and organizing ability. As he saw it, the "contrabands" had to be not only fed, clothed, and set to work, but also given the rudiments of an education and taught the moral standards of a free society.

Eaton was later made a brevetted brigadier general for the excellent work he did in this position. And later still, in 1870, he became United States commissioner of education. He headed the United States Bureau of Education until 1886, when he accepted the presidency of Marietta College. His last position was that of inspector of education in Puerto Rico, where he must have found use for much that he had learned during the war years.

If we may judge by his choice of Samuel Thomas to take care of the Vicksburg area, one of Eaton's many gifts was his ability to find men to act as his aides who were in sympathy with his aims. And it was Vicksburg's good fortune that the chaplain of the resident Negro regiment was also such a man. Both Warren and Thomas felt so much genuine concern for the southern Negro that they continued to work on his behalf after the war. Colonel Thomas, who had held the rank of assistant commissioner under Eaton, was on Eaton's recommendation put in charge of the Freedmen's Bureau for Mississippi when it was established just before the end of the war, and Dr. Joseph Warren was appointed superintendent of education for freedmen in Mississippi.

Colonel Thomas was the man really responsible for the earlier decision of Messrs. Morgan and McKee to locate the United Brethren Mission in Vicksburg. He had welcomed the idea of a school and had secured from the army permission to furnish housing for the classes and for the Mission personnel as well as some supplies for the proposed work.

The housing assigned to the Morgans and the three young teachers was the second floor of the large building already mentioned. On the first floor, in addition to the offices for work concerned with the Negroes, were quarters for some of the Negro soldiers. Sarah Dickey told a story about one of her first nights in the building. She had scarcely noticed a hole in the chimney that ran through her room. It seemed just part of the general disrepair. But when on this night flames began to shoot out of it, she acted with characteristic vigor. Seizing a bucket of water she managed to put out what she thought was a fire in the chimney. Not till later did she learn of the dismay felt by a group of shivering soldiers quartered in the room below who with difficulty had collected enough wood to make a fire to take the chill off the cold December night, only to have their promising blaze effectually quenched by a deluge from above. William McKee in a letter home told of the scarcity of fuel — even wooden sidewalks and fences were torn up and used in the absence of coal or cordwood.

Sarah Dickey used to describe other experiences in this building in which she lived for the nineteen months of her stay in Vicksburg. It had a reputation as a haunted house. Occasionally in the night, she said, they would hear sounds as though someone with a cane were dragging himself painfully along, a reminiscence, perhaps, of the building's hospital days. They never could satisfactorily account for the sounds. More to be feared, however, than a wounded ghost was the very real possibility of a surprise attack from some of General Forrest's roving troops. When he was known to be in the general vicinity, they kept their belongings packed, ready to make a dash to shelter within the fortifications.

It was on a Friday that she and her fellow workers had landed. After meeting Colonel Thomas and Chaplain Warren, the three young women and Mrs. Morgan, who was to take care of the housekeeping, put in the rest of the day and all day Saturday in a perfect frenzy of cleaning. The place had had almost no attention since the makeshift hospital had been given up. Their energy and thoroughness were something new in that part of the world and startled all beholders. By Sunday their living quarters were spotlessly clean and, thanks to the arrangement of their personal belongings, even homelike. On Sunday they doubtless went to church services, and it is to be hoped that they rested, for on the next day they began their teaching.

"The young ladies take the school by storm," wrote Mr. McKee in his last letter from Vicksburg. He put the school entirely in their hands and departed to start another mission down the river where at Davis Bend a promising experiment was being tried. The "young ladies" must have experienced a sinking of the heart, not at being left in charge but at the place in which they were to teach. It was not where the school had been started. This experience of being moved was a first taste for the Mission of the uncertainty and insecurity of dealing with changing military commands, conditions which in less than three years led to giving up the Mission altogether. The school had been started with General McArthur's permission in the basement of a Methodist church. But though the Methodists in town were willing that Sunday services for Negroes should be held in their former church, they objected to the idea of using any part of it as a school for them. Other denominations felt the same way. Was it that they thought a church building should be used only for religious purposes or that they feared education would make their ex-slaves harder to deal with? Whatever their reason, the military command of the city respected it and ordered the United Brethren Mission to get another location for its school.

Finally a Baptist church on the corner of Crawford and Walnut was made available. It had been vacated by its members when Union troops took it over and occupied it during the last days of the siege. Under direct attacks the church had suffered; all the windows were shattered and the doors unhinged; the wind had easy access. It was a drafty, uncomfortable place. Bloodstains on the floor and a shell hole in the wall through which a badly wounded soldier had crawled were reminders of the recent past. Two small stoves in the big room were poor defense against the damp cold of the winter months.

Here Sarah Dickey, Ettie Stubbs, and Minnie Hanson organized their school. They did not wait for the promised repairs, which in the unsettled state of everything could not be counted on. They chose the three most sheltered places for their classes, two of them on either side of the pulpit. It is hard to imagine how they managed, yet manage they did; for from the May 1864 report of the work sent North, we learn that the Negroes flocked to the school, three hundred of them, and that in spite of irregular attendance they studied hard and learned rapidly. Quoting from the report:

When school first opened there were not a dozen who could read or one who could write. Since then, about one hundred have been taught to read readily in the New Testament. About fifty of this number have made good proficiency in penmanship, geography, English grammar and arithmetic.

The report also speaks of improvement in manners, personal cleanliness, and the like. The enrollment fee of fifteen cents must have presented a considerable obstacle to many, for under conditions then existing in Vicksburg there was little opportunity to earn even fifteen cents. That so many managed to enroll testifies to the strength of their desire for education.

Teaching the three R's was by no means the whole of Sarah Dickey's work. She was asked to help in straightening out the marital relationships among the Negroes. Legal marriage and marriage certificates were nothing that slaves had had dealing with. They might possibly have had as many different husbands or wives as they had had masters, for when they were sold usually no account was made of their families. Now John Eaton and his aides were trying to bring some sort of order out of the resultant chaos. They insisted on a regular marriage complete with marriage certificate. Dealing with such numbers — more than three thousand marriages were performed in Vicksburg during eight months of 1864 — Chaplain Warren and other officiating chaplains were obliged to marry the couples in job lots, a dozen or so with a single pronouncement of the marriage lines, each marriage properly attested to by a marriage certificate. Sarah Dickey was one of those who made out the certificates and had them ready for the chaplain to sign. When she had a sufficient number made out, she would send for him, gather the couples about her and, while they were waiting, talk to them about the Christian ideal of marriage, its sacredness and obligations. In this work she came to understand something of the many difficulties the freedmen faced in their new and rapidly changing environment, something also of their yearnings and high hopes, of their disappointments, too, and much of the ways in which their background of servitude had conditioned them.

In getting names for the certificates she encountered the same difficulty she had met in registering students — that of surnames. The field hands for the most part could offer only the names by which they were called — Dick, Minnie, Lizzie, Joe. House servants and workmen might give their last master's name as their surname, their mother's or their father's name or, occasionally, a place name and, to confuse matters more, now one name, now another.

Sunday was no day of rest for the teachers. Two church services and a growing Sunday school kept all the Mission busy. Right after Christmas, less than three weeks from the time of Sarah Dickey's arrival, a United Brethren church with 97 members was organized. By the first of May when a report was sent North, the church membership had grown to 397 and regular attendance at Sunday school to 175.

The week of the founding of the church, that is, the week between Christmas and New Year's day in 1863, and also that same week in 1864, were the only weeks in the nineteen months that Sarah Dickey taught at Vicksburg in which the day school was not held, and she was the only one of the entire staff who never missed a day. Indeed there was a time in the searing heat of the summer of 1864, record heat even for Mississippi, when there were only three to carry on all the work of the Mission, she and Rev. Mr. and Mrs. William Otterbein Grimm, who had been sent to take charge of the work when Mr. Morgan's health began to fail. We get an idea of the teaching work of the Mission from the following entry in a report dated May 9, 1865: "About 700 persons, including soldiers, were under instruction during the year, many of whom made commendable progress in study."

This report also recounted the serious housing trouble the Mission had labored under. A year earlier General McPherson had sent a military order for turning over the Baptist church where they taught to the agent of the Baptist Mission Association who was in Vicksburg. This meant that the United Brethren must have a building they could call their own. Chaplain Warren, canvassing possible sites for them, chose one with as good a title as possible. Through him and Colonel Thomas they received government promise of timber for the building. The church members were enthusiastic about the project and agreed to help in the construction as well as to raise funds for it. But month succeeded month as one military emergency after another made it impossible for the government teams to haul the logs and the government sawmill to saw them. The freedmen became discouraged and began to lose interest. It was evident that the Mission must build immediately if it was to continue. So lumber was purchased at considerable expense and shipped down the river. At last, in the spring of 1865, Sarah Dickey and the others happily moved into their own building, a building well suited to the needs of both church and school.

Much had happened in those months of doubt and uncertainty. The Grimms had arrived, the Morgans had left and after a rest had returned, Minnie Hanson, seriously ill with typhoid fever, had also gone North for a time. On her return she devoted herself to teaching the soldiers, members of the 66th United States Colored Infantry. At the close of the war she continued her work, traveling with them until they were mustered out in Natchez, March 20, 1866. During part of this time, perhaps because of lack of schoolroom space or perhaps because of the great need, Ettie Stubbs did what we now call social work. She visited the miserable hovels where the poorer freedmen lived, trying to help in various ways. Sometimes she found as many as six of them living in a windowless hut not more than six feet square. These conditions Sarah Dickey, too, saw at first hand. In the unusual heat of that summer of 1864, they all suffered and one of their number died. She was Mary Stewart of Flat Rock, Ohio, who with William McKee had joined the Vicksburg group when the Davis Bend Mission had to be given up.

During all these comings and goings, the illnesses, the terrific heat, the moves from place to place, the heartbreaking disappointments about the building, Sarah Dickey went on uninterruptedly with her teaching. Perhaps what bore her up was an experience she had had soon after her arrival in Vicksburg. It was her old dream of wandering in a wood, but this time with a difference. When she came to the edge of the wood where the great wall had been, and we quote her own account, "A voice seemed to say to me 'Where is that wall?' and I opened my eyes and looked, but it was gone, and I realized that I was in the field that I had seen beyond the wall so long." She had no doubt as to the significance of this experience. The work she was doing, or work like it, was to be her life work. She threw herself wholeheartedly into it, demanding and exhausting though it was, for she knew she was under divine guidance.

Once settled in their own building, the mission workers felt that their troubles were over. Though by now there were other missions in the field also doing good work, the need far exceeded the number of helpers. The report that went North looked to "a great harvest to be gathered." They awaited eagerly the end of the dreadful war, an end that seemed to be approaching. But when it came, with Lee's surrender to Grant at Appomatox on April 8, 1865, a change in military command and a consequent change in policy at Vicksburg dealt the Mission a death blow. The military authorities decided to give back to its original owner the land on which the United Brethren Mission at so much expense and effort had built their church and school. Ordered to remove their building as soon as possible and finding no land with a reasonably clear title to which to move it, those in charge reluctantly decided to close the Vicksburg Mission. The fact that the government was planning to take over the education of the freedmen and that Dr. Joseph Warren was appointed under the Freedmen's Bureau as superintendent of freedmen's schools in Mississippi made giving up the teaching end of their Mission easier. The Grimms would stay on to wind up affairs. Late spring or early summer saw Sarah Dickey on her way North.

For her personally, the end of the Vicksburg experience was

no calamity. It gave her the opportunity to do what she had increasingly felt the need of, to educate herself further for her life work. Both in her own mission and elsewhere she had come to know people who had richer, fuller backgrounds than hers, many of them college educated people. Did she appraise her own background as limited and provincial and feel the need of more and better education? She has not told us her reasoning, only her determination to somehow get the best education available to prepare herself for her life work.

The nineteen months in Vicksburg had been one kind of preparation, too, invaluable preparation. They had given her an understanding of the people with whom she intended to spend her life. She knew their warm friendliness, their hopes and desires, their patience, their loyalty, their many frustrations, their many handicaps, their special problems, and their great need. She had become acquainted with the Southern scene and had learned to live and work with a variety of people. What she needed now was more education.

2.   The First Goal

A DIFFICULTY in trying to follow the movements of a single-minded person like Sarah Dickey is that the object of the study offers no assistance except along the line of that person's central interest. So unless there are bystanders to fill in the gaps, the biographer is helpless. No bystander has come forward to tell us of Sarah Dickey's trip North after her nineteen months in Vicksburg or of her visit in Middletown, Ohio, to see her father and perhaps other relatives there and in Dayton where she went to report in person to her Mission Board. It is not till she reached Richmond, Indiana, that we have any firsthand information. She had gone to Richmond to consult with her sister, Mrs. Mather, the only member of her family who had any sympathy with her desire for more education or the use she planned to make of it. It is reported of her only brother that he had thought of setting her up with a house and lot until he heard about her silly idea of spending money on more schooling.

Not that she had any money to spend. The lack of it was her trouble. She needed to find a place where she could work for the privilege of studying. When in Middletown she may very possibly have tried to enter Western Female Seminary in nearby Oxford, known now as Western College. It would have served her well had she been able to go there. The teachers, largely Mount Holyoke women, had given it an excellent reputation. Mount Holyoke trained teachers were in great demand and pretty well scattered through the northern and central states. Her sister had had one whom she greatly admired.

She and Sarah regretted the distance that separated them from that most highly regarded institution. "If only you could go to Mount Holyoke Seminary, Sarah," her sister had once said. But

19

clearly she could not go such a distance. They put the idea out of their minds and turned their thoughts to schools within reach. Right there in Richmond was Earlham College, a Quaker co-educational school. It is the only one that we know she tried to enter, for she mentions no other names, saying only that she tried in vain at several. It was in vain at Earlham, too, but something else came of her interview there. Those she talked with, evidently arrested by something about her and hearing of her Vicksburg experience and her desire to continue teaching the freedmen, passed her on to other Friends in the Richmond Quaker center. The result was that they offered to send her South to their mission for the freedmen.

This offer posed a problem for her. She had tried without success to gain entrance to institutions within reach. Nowhere did there seem to be a place for an unknown, penniless student, however willing she was to work. Already twenty-seven, was she too old as well as too poor to get that much-wanted further education? Now she was offered an opportunity for the very work to which she felt the Lord had called her. Obviously the sensible thing was to accept the offer; yet something within her rebelled. She tells of her struggle and its outcome in an account written thirty-six years later. It appeared in a little paper called *The Dew of Hermon* (see Chapter VII).

. . . I made up my mind that I should just stop trying to do the impossible, do the best I could with what education I had. But as soon as I decided on that course, my whole being was stirred to the very depth and I could not rest day or night. So one day when I was doing some work in a room alone and my heart was so burdened, I just stood up straight and said: "Lord, what *shall* I do?" And just as quickly as the words could be spoken, in the same decided tone, the answer came: "Go to Mt. Holyoke Seminary!" It seemed to me like an audible voice. Without another thought I just pressed my foot on the floor and said: *"Go to Mt. Holyoke Seminary, that I will!"* And when I said it I could command but ten dollars in the world.

And go to Mount Holyoke she did, as later she accomplished other apparently impossible things once she was convinced that they were God's will for her. The decision made, she went forward with never a backward glance. She borrowed money

from her church, which had every reason to believe in one who
had given such valiant service. Within two weeks she had embarked on the long train journey east.

It was not an easy journey. For one thing she had not thought
to provide herself with food for the trip like some of her fellow
passengers nor did she have money to buy any, like the rest. So
for thirty-four hours she had nothing to eat. A more serious
difficulty met her at Albany. Her ticket took her only that far
because the town where the Seminary was located, South Hadley, was not on a railroad and the ticket agent at Richmond was
therefore uncertain about the further route. At Albany, he told
her, she would be reliably directed and could purchase the rest
of her ticket. He was right in part. At Albany she received
clear instructions. She was to go from Albany to Springfield,
change cars there for a train that went north along the west
bank of the Connecticut River, get off at a station called Smiths
Ferry where there would be a ferry to take her across the river
to a waiting stage for South Hadley and Mount Holyoke Seminary. The agent had been explicit and kind, but when he found
that the young woman did not have enough money left to pay
for her train ticket, let alone ferry and stage, he brusquely told
her that she had no business to start if she could not complete
her journey. Rebuffed, she retreated to the waiting room and
there prayed for guidance in this emergency. While she was
praying, the ticket agent had a change of heart. He came to her
with a plan. He would advance the fare if she would leave her
trunk as collateral. Probably the fact that she was going to
Mount Holyoke Seminary counted largely with him. The reputation of the place and of the people in charge gave him
assurance that he would be repaid.

So Sarah Dickey was able to continue her journey as directed
and eventually found herself crossing the Connecticut River on
a craft that seemed strange to her after the Mississippi River
boats she had known. One of her classmates has left a description of the ferry as it was then — flat-bottomed and open, large
enough to take two teams of horses and considerable freight
with standing room for a good many passengers. It was pro-

pelled by two men who walked slowly up and down its length lifting a cable from the river and pulling on it with something that looked, she wrote, like nothing so much as a curry comb.

The open stage on the other side carried Sarah Dickey the short mile to the village. South Hadley is not one of the old New England towns. It had been settled little more than a hundred years when Sarah Dickey arrived, but at least it had a small green, a beautiful white, colonial-style church and comfortable-looking white frame houses set back from the road. The stage deposited her a short distance south of the green before a large, four-story, light-colored brick building. Its appearance is familiar from copies of the Currier lithograph of it. We see it only as a quaint period piece, but to Sarah Dickey, looking for the first time at the building where all her desires were centered, it must have seemed like something out of the New Jerusalem. It contained all she had hoped for and dreamed about. Though exhausted from her long journey and faint from lack of food, she thought only of her need to become a member of the charmed community which it housed.

That she became a member of the community is one of those minor miracles which mark her course through life. She had arrived after the beginning of the fall term, and the few opportunities for a student to earn her way were already taken. What could Mrs. Stoddard, the new acting principal, have thought when this travel-worn, penniless young woman presented herself and explained that she had come from Indiana to enroll in the four-year course at Mount Holyoke Seminary? Fortunately for Mrs. Stoddard, the former principal was there visiting for a few days. Until her marriage less than six months earlier, Mary M. Chapin, now Mrs. Pease, had been principal of the Seminary for fifteen years and before that a teacher in it from the year after her graduation in 1843. Mrs. Stoddard called Mrs. Pease in for consultation. Together they heard Sarah Dickey's story. Questioning brought out additional facts: that Miss Dickey knew no one in the Seminary nor in all New England; that she had no money except for the thirty-four cents in her purse nor prospect of getting any except by working; that she was in debt for money borrowed for her trip east as well as to the ticket agent in Albany. The matter of the ticket agent was at least something they could act on immediately. Mrs. Pease agreed to send the necessary amount and ask that Miss Dickey's trunk be forwarded. Further than that there was little they could offer at the moment. They did say, however, that while she was waiting for her trunk and living with them in the Seminary, Miss Dickey might take the required entrance examinations. There were still two weeks left during which they were offered. Then, if she passed them and a way should open for her to stay, she would be ready to enroll.

By the final day she had passed all the required examinations — Latin, English grammar, United States history, modern geography, and mathematics. This last included mental and written arithmetic and algebra through simple equations. She worked especially hard on the Latin. Her Vicksburg experience had pretty well erased what little Latin she had acquired in those pre-Vicksburg years of alternate study and teaching.

Close on the arrival of her trunk came the minor miracle. One of the three students who had been given the opportunity to work their way through the school year had been called home and would not be able to return. Miss Dickey might have her place. The position involved three-and-a-half hours of work in the Seminary on the four recitation days and more time on Wednesday, the recreation day, and on Saturday, the composition day — a heavy load to carry with the regular studies.

Nor was this all of the miracle. Though the work expected of her would cover the cost of tuition, board and room, it did not cover the heating and lighting of that room. She and the roommate she would have must share the cost of the coal they burned in their open Franklin stove and of the kerosene for their study lamps. She would also need money to buy the required textbooks, to pay certain regular fees to cover her share in expeditions taken in connection with certain courses, and her own support during the two short vacations, two weeks each, that separated the fall from the winter term and the winter from the last term of the school year. In the longer summer vacation she could earn money toward the expenses of the next year. For the extra expenses of this year they had decided, Mrs. Stoddard told her, to let her have the sixty dollars that a kind gentleman had left them when the pupil for whom the money was intended had not been able to stay. Thus it came about that within a month of receiving what she recognized as God's command, Sarah Dickey, the cost of her first year assured, was enrolled as a member of the class of 1869 in Mount Holyoke Female Seminary.

That we know so much about what took place during her seminary course is due to a remarkable record preserved in the Mount Holyoke College archives. It is called the *Seminary Journal* and was kept for more than forty years, now by this teacher, now by that. Handwritten copies were sent to former students at work in foreign lands to keep them in touch with their alma mater, and later sent also to some nearer home. Later still they were printed, but that was after Sarah Dickey's time. These journal letters, like family letters sent to absent members, tell of matters big and little that might be of interest to one who is far from a well-loved home. For instance, from that part of the *Seminary Journal* covering Sarah Dickey's first half year we learn that the 1865 Indian summer was late and unusually lovely; that on the day the writer made the entry, she was planning to go to the woods for partridge berries, fern and moss; that the new gymnasium was finished and much admired though apparatus was still lacking; that three cases of typhoid fever had developed, a teacher and two students, and that one of the students had died, saddening them all; that a New York City man through the influence of a trustee had sent them a box of books for the library that included eleven volumes of the Audubon plates; that of the sixty-eight students who at the beginning of the fall term had declared themselves "without hope," twenty-one had been converted by the end of the term; that Dr. Mead, pastor of the village church and a trustee of the Seminary, was enjoying a needed holiday in Europe; that on Christmas day Professor Brackett from Bowdoin College delivered his first lecture on chemistry and for the next three

weeks gave two lectures a day, one on chemistry and one on
geology, keeping them all very busy; that on the evening of the
same Christmas day, at a gay party in the parlors, Cornelius, the
genial Irishman who did the heavy work about the place,
dressed in buffalo robes and hung about with presents, played
the part of Santa Claus and distributed the gifts. There were
other items, of course, but these are enough to give an idea of
their interest and variety.

Except for a few gaps in the record, we can pretty well re-
construct the life in the Seminary during Sarah Dickey's four
years. There is even one mention of her. It occurs in her senior
year and reads "May 28, 1869 — Miss Dickey received news
of her father's death." Teachers are always mentioned by name
in the *Seminary Journal,* but students so rarely that this mention
stands out. Has it some special significance? At least it shows
that by her last year "Miss Dickey" was well enough known for
the item to have some general interest. We, on our side, aware
of her devotion to her father, know what a crushing blow this
was. Coming as it did less than two months before her graduation, it cast a shadow over that event.

But the most important thing that happened to her during
her Holyoke years was unknown to the journalist or to anyone
else until in her last year she confided in one of the teachers.
It had happened almost at the beginning of her seminary life
and was the determining factor in her future. Here is her own
account of it written years later in that same *Dew of Hermon*
already referred to:

When I had been at the Seminary about four weeks that same familiar
voice said: "This is what the Lord wants you to do in the South: to
build a Seminary like this for the colored girls." To that I answered,
"No, that could not be the voice of God, for I certainly never could do
such a work as that."

Clearly she was profoundly disturbed. Always before the
voice had directed her along the line of her own subconscious
desires — coming to Mount Holyoke, for instance. Deep within,
she was uneasy. Could it be that this impossible task was expected of her? She fought the idea until late in her senior year.

She tried to replace it with her old plan of becoming a missionary in Africa. With her Vicksburg experience behind her and her Mount Holyoke connections, she was in no danger of being refused again. She tells us that when in her third year a moving plea was made for immediate help in a South African mission, all that kept her from volunteering on the spot was her conviction that since God had sent her to Mount Holyoke, He must expect her to finish the course. Then she could go. She reasoned that because she would be working for the same race in Africa as in the South, God would be just as well pleased. Yet in spite of such reasoning, she says, "The thought of the work in the South would not leave me."

Undoubtedly this idea of a Mount Holyoke for colored girls in the South, planted so early in her four years of study, alerted her to much about the seminary life and work that she might not otherwise have thought about or even noticed. She was both consciously and unconsciously accumulating a storehouse of knowledge and experience that served her well in later years.

Her most obvious indebtedness was to Mount Holyoke's famous domestic work system. Mary Lyon had instituted it nearly thirty years earlier in order to reduce the cost of an education. It still served that purpose though the cost had risen by Sarah Dickey's time from $60.00 a year to $125 and in her third year was further raised to $150.00. Except for the services of the already mentioned Cornelius, all the work was done by the students. Yet no student spent more than one hour a day at her appointed task unless, like Sarah Dickey, she was earning her way. With three terms in a school year and assignments usually made for one term, both continuity and variety of work were assured. From the students' point of view, the best feature of the plan was that many of the tasks were assigned not to individuals but to groups called circles. The girls could have fun together talking and laughing as they worked. To some of the circles they gave identifying names such as the Blue Crockery Circle for those who washed the willow-ware dishes and the Black Artillery Circle for those who dealt with pots and pans.

To ensure the smooth running of such an intricate system,

there had to be, of course, rules and regulations — too many
of them it seems to us today. Some of the students of those days
thought so too. Nonetheless they appear to have accomplished
their purpose with a minimum of friction. An ingenious system
of self-reporting kept them well in mind. For example, there
were rules about promptness. The need for them is clear. Sarah
Dickey later made a great point of punctuality in her own
school. At Mount Holyoke it was enforced by these questions
asked daily: Has anyone been tardy at school exercises? at
recitations? at meals? for her domestic work? in going to bed?
When a student pleaded guilty to any of these sins, she was
asked how many minutes late she had been, and the number
was duly recorded along with the "exception," as any infraction
of a rule was called. The public shame of too many exceptions
seems to have been sufficient punishment.

Though these arrangements appear regimented and discipli-
nary, their final effect was something very different. Indeed, the
principals and teachers responsible for organizing and supervising the daily household tasks of nearly three hundred students, exhausting as they found it, heartily believed in the
domestic work system. Their espousal was not so much for its
original economic purpose, which it still served, as for the sense
of home and family that was developed by working together
for common needs. The Seminary was referred to more often
as "home" than "school." The very existence of the *Seminary
Journal* is proof that those far away still belonged to and cared
about the place.

To Sarah Dickey this sense of being a member of the seminary family meant a great deal. From the time of her mother's
death she had had no real experience of family life. Here at
Mount Holyoke she became an integral part in the life of the
Seminary, sharing its interests and responsibilities. It was a
place where she "belonged" and to which in later years she
returned again and again as she did to her church home in
Dayton, Ohio. These two places were precious to her throughout her life.

This analogy of the Seminary to a family and home is not a

forced one. The life at Mount Holyoke in those days ran a considerable gamut of shared family experience, and not just in the ordinary details of daily living. When students were ill — as they often were in those days before much was known about modern sanitation — they were usually cared for in the Seminary by the resident doctor and the teachers. Hence most of the students knew of the illnesses and felt a common concern. Occasionally an epidemic would strike. In the spring of Sarah Dickey's second year the physician, Dr. Emily Belden, had to turn one wing of the Seminary into an improvised hospital for thirty cases of measles. Influenza followed. One day there were fifty on the sick list. It may be that the skill Sarah Dickey later showed in treating illness in her school came from helping Dr. Belden and some of the teachers at this difficult time. Because she was so much older than most of the students she might very possibly have been called on to help in such an emergency.

Romance played its more agreeable part in the seminary family life. Since the distant readers of the *Seminary Journal* would not be acquainted with most of the undergraduates, their romances are not reported. But scarcely a year went by without mention of at least one teacher, and usually more, leaving at the end of the year to be married. Nor were they always the younger ones. Of the six principals who followed Mary Lyon, four resigned to make homes of their own. Such incidents enlivened seminary life. Teachers and students would sew for the brides-to-be and give them farewell parties and presents — and not only for them but also for those equally romantic figures who had pledged themselves to mission work overseas or in the far west. We read that at the departure of some missionaries-elect the students crowded the piazzas to sing to them and wave a final farewell as they drove off. How wholeheartedly Sarah Dickey must have joined in such scenes!

There were usually even some children in the seminary family, for the steward, with his family, always lived in the building. In Sarah Dickey's first year this was Mr. Chapin (Mrs. Pease's brother) and family.

If the lack of a father and a plethora of mothers somewhat

invalidate the analogy to a family, the parental part played by some of the trustees should be remembered. One room in the Seminary was called Deacon Porter's room, reserved for him on his many business visits. He was often accompanied by Mrs. Porter, a great favorite with the students. In Sarah Dickey's last two years a newly appointed trustee, Mr. Henry Durant, later founder of Wellesley College, was another who spent a good deal of time at Mount Holyoke, frequently with his wife who was equally concerned for the Seminary's welfare. Mr. Durant was especially interested in the religious life of the students, conducting services and talking to the girls individually. We read also of the unexpected and welcome gifts sent by the Durants — boxes of oranges, a fruit rare in the North at that time, oysters, too, and on one occasion, 150 boxes of strawberries.

The many guests who came and went in an almost constant stream testify to the hospitable, homelike atmosphere of the place. Students as well as teachers felt themselves to be in some measure hostesses. Besides trustees with or without their wives, the guests included visiting ministers, missionaries — many of them alumnae with interesting stories to tell of life in foreign parts — other former students, visitors come to study the school of which they had heard so much, speakers on a wide range of subjects, and those regular lecturers engaged to supplement the work of a course, some of them staying in the Seminary for weeks at a time.

The family feeling is further evidenced by the interest the students took in the appearance and comfort of their seminary home. A group of them who thought one of the parlors needed a new carpet made up a purse and with a teacher went to Springfield to select one to their liking.

Then there was the gymnasium. One of the first things Sarah Dickey would have been told on her arrival when all were admiring the new, steam-heated gymnasium was the pleasant story of how it happened. A student was responsible for its being built at that particular time. Because this student had felt the need of a gymnasium for Mount Holyoke so keenly and had presented that need with such eloquence and logic in one of the essays read at her graduating exercises two years earlier, the governor of Massachusetts, John A. Andrew, in the audience at the time, started a subscription for the building on the spot. By the end of the day almost two thousand dollars had been pledged. The cautious trustees, long aware of the need but not feeling justified in adding to the seminary debt, yielded to the pressure of such popular demand. Is it any wonder that the students felt special pride in the new gymnasium?

That building in its turn was indirectly responsible for yet another improvement. The comforting warmth of the steam heat made teachers and students alike think about the possibility of steam heat for the main building. Their own rooms were snug and warm with their small, open-front stoves, but the long halls — spaceways, they called them — were cold and drafty. In winter the girls kept their shawls on pegs by the door to wrap around themselves for the dash through the chill corridors to their various appointments. The trustees, when they were consulted, refused to consider further borrowing. They already had a $27,000 debt on their hands. However, they did yield to the faculty request that they at least get an estimate of what steam heat for the building would cost. This was in Sarah Dickey's third year and she was doubtless present at a history-making meeting of teachers and students. The amount of the estimate was announced, ten thousand dollars, and they decided to undertake raising the money themselves. All joined the campaign. The following excerpt from a teacher's letter under the date of November 20, 1867 tells of that beginning:

The engineers report that ten thousand dollars will cover the expense for putting steam in every room, and we teachers and scholars have resolved to try to raise the money ourselves. There is great enthusiasm on the subject. Hundreds of letters have been written within a week, asking aid from graduates and others. Most of us mean to see what we can do personally in vacation. We do not intend to refuse any sum, from ten cents to a thousand dollars! . . . Yesterday the mercury stood at fourteen degrees below zero.

The vacation referred to was the one between the fall and

winter terms, only eight days away. Vacation efforts resulted in nine hundred dollars being added to the fund.

Excitement ran high. For fifteen consecutive weeks every mail brought some contribution and every evening the sum was recorded and the total made known. The leanest day brought only a dollar and a half; the best, two hundred and twenty-seven dollars. A barrel of apples donated to the cause netted twenty dollars when the apples were sold by the piece at a New Year's party. The weather, too, was cooperative, the winter unusually long and cold. As one letter put it, "If our zeal wavers, we have only to pass a little way through the freezing halls to get fresh impetus." The largest single gift, and there were not many of that figure, was one hundred dollars. But the alumnae made up in numbers what most of them lacked in purse. By the end of the winter term, the fund stood at $4,680.00. Though the active work on the project ended at that time, contributions kept coming in until by graduation time more than half of the needed amount had been raised. Sarah Dickey would have learned a good deal about personal solicitation from hearing the experiences of others, even if she herself could take little part in the work, and she saw the way many small contributions mount up to a considerable sum.

The reason for giving up further solicitation at the end of the winter term was a third attempt on the part of the trustees to get a grant from the Massachusetts State Legislature. The colleges of Amherst, Tufts, Williams and the Massachusetts Agricultural College, as well as Wilbraham Academy, had all received grants from the State of from $10,000 to $50,000. Mount Holyoke had applied in vain in 1864 and again in 1866. War conditions and the fact that some legislators thought it wasteful to spend money on the education of women were both reasons for the refusals. This third appeal in 1868 was for $40,000. The students eagerly followed every step. The application had to be approved by the Committee on Finance and the Committee on Education before it could be presented to the two houses of the legislature — a slow process. Miss French, who had succeeded Mrs. Stoddard as principal when the latter

left to be married again, was twice called to Boston, first to
consult with the Committee on Finance and then, a month later,
with the Committee on Education. On their return she and
those she took with her told the students about their interviews.
Hopes ran high when the two committees recommended the
grant to the legislature. Finally, at supper on May 14, 1868,
Miss French read a letter she had just received announcing the
passage of the bill. As the governor's signature was assured,
students and teachers alike could scarcely contain themselves
for joy. Their expression took the form of an illumination. As
soon as it was dark, they placed lights in every window of the
great building and in the cupola. All poured outdoors to see
the sight and to wander around the grounds in jubilant groups,
often breaking into song. They wound up the evening by gath-
ering under the principal's window and singing "Praise God
from whom all blessings flow."

There was ample reason for rejoicing. The forty thousand
dollars not only wiped out the seminary debt and completed the
amount needed for the steam heat, but it made possible going
ahead with plans for a fireproof library. Mrs. Durant had
promised ten thousand dollars for books if a fireproof building
to house them was built within three years.

All these shared interests connected with their seminary home
brought the students and teachers into an unusually close relationship. For the most part they even shared a common social
life. Such sharing was the more natural because so many of the
teachers were young. In Sarah Dickey's first year, for instance,
three-fourths of the teachers had graduated at most not more
than five years earlier, and one that very year. This high proportion of young teachers had been characteristic of the Seminary from the beginning.

Officially also students and teachers were thrown together in
a rather special way. The students were divided into groups of
twenty called sections. Each section was in the care of a teacher
who was to act as older sister and friend. She had plenty of
other duties as well, such as keeping a full record of each of
her twenty charges. It was to her that they made their daily

report of "exceptions." Other pages in her section book were devoted to domestic work, time spent on compositions, words misspelled, Bible lessons and wardrobe inspection. What we find referred to in students' letters of the time, however, is not this routine record keeping, but a daily fifteen minute "recess meeting" in the section teacher's own room. Starting as prayer groups, these short meetings had come to be used in whatever way the section teacher thought best. Such informal meetings go far to explain the warm affection with which the section teacher was generally regarded. "Blessed little recess meetings," one student ejaculated in a letter home. We read also of tramps and picnics together. A young section teacher wrote of leading her section up Mount Holyoke and not getting back until after nine o'clock at night. "Nobody was lost, and we had a splendid time." Sarah Dickey does not say who her section teachers were. We might hazard a guess that one of them could have been Miss Anna C. Edwards, with whom she corresponded later, and another, Miss Julia Ward, to whom she went for advice in her senior year. Whoever they were, they played an important part in the family life of the Seminary, a life that meant much to Sarah Dickey.

3. Mount Holyoke, 1865 - 1869

FAMILY LIFE as developed at Mount Holyoke was largely a homemade product that served its purpose well and was a useful model for various "daughter" schools such as Lake Erie and Western in Ohio and Mills in California. But the education such a system aimed to bring within reach of young women of moderate means was not homemade. It was based as closely as circumstances permitted on that offered in colleges for men. By examining the 1865 to 1869 catalogues of a few small New England colleges and comparing the courses of study outlined with the course at Mount Holyoke, we get an idea of the education Sarah Dickey received in relation to her time. Amherst, Williams, Dartmouth, and Bowdoin are the colleges chosen for this comparison. But first certain matters common to them all and to Mount Holyoke should be kept in mind: required courses were the order of the day; in only two of the colleges do we find the first faint flutter of an elective. Most of the courses were term courses, not year courses, and the school year was more than two months longer than it is today: forty weeks for Mount Holyoke; thirty-nine and thirty-eight for the others. The minimum age for entrance at the colleges was fifteen years; at Mount Holyoke, sixteen.

The most striking fact that emerges from our comparison is that the greatest difference between the work offered at the Seminary and at the colleges appears in the first two years and the greatest likeness in the last two, especially in the senior year. The work of the first two years in the colleges was so given over to courses in Greek and Latin — sometimes as many as five were taken in a single term — that there was room for little else except mathematics. At Mount Holyoke, on the other

34

hand, no Greek was given and the Latin, though required for
entrance and throughout the four years, was more elementary.
Mathematics too was less extensive; algebra, Euclid, and trigo-
nometry were required respectively in the first three years. Consequently there was space, especially in the first year, for more
variety. For instance, in that year Sarah Dickey, in addition to
reading Sallust, studied Latin prose composition and algebra,
reviewed English grammar, took two science courses as well as
courses in ancient history and in ancient geography which put
the story of the Jews into a world context of time and place.
The work in Bible that first year took up the books of Genesis
and Exodus.

Another difference, and one to be regretted, was not limited
to any particular year. It was the absence at Mount Holyoke
of regular work in any modern language. French could be had
as an extra. Under the heading "Instruction is also given" we
find listed vocal music, drawing, penmanship and French, all
of them reminiscent of the popular "finishing" schools. At the
colleges, however, work was given in one or two modern languages. French, German, Italian and Spanish all appear in one
or another of the institutions, although in the few terms
assigned to their study one wonders if more than an elementary
reading knowledge could have been acquired.

When we look at the studies of the last two years we find a
change in focus. In the colleges the courses in classics, less
numerous in the third year, disappear entirely as required work
in the fourth. The history of English literature makes a modest
debut in that same year; it had appeared at the Seminary a year
earlier. But the real center of the work, especially in the senior
year, was in more abstract, speculative and religious subjects.
A course called Evidences of Christianity appears in all five
curricula; one on Wayland's *Elements of Moral Science* was
given at the Seminary and at Bowdoin and Amherst. Mental
Philosophy appears at Bowdoin and Mount Holyoke, Intellectual Philosophy at Williams and Moral Philosophy at Dartmouth!
A course required in the senior year at all the colleges and at
the Seminary was on a text written a hundred years earlier but

still studied at Cambridge and Oxford and at most self-respecting American colleges of the time. It was Bishop Butler's *Analogy of Religion, Natural and Revealed, to the Constitution and Course of Nature,* popularly known as "Butler's Analogy." The classics and mathematics of the early years had little bearing on such courses, but work in the sciences provided valuable background for them. The continued attempt at rapprochement between science and religion, implicit in some of the above course titles, was of importance to colleges built, as these colleges had been, on a religious foundation.

The college students had had the necessary background work in science. So, too, had those at Mount Holyoke, thanks to Mary Lyon. Her keen interest in science and her friendship with Edward Hitchcock, science professor at Amherst College and later its president, had resulted in special attention to scientific studies at the Seminary from its beginning. By Sarah Dickey's time physiology and Gray's Botany were required in the first year; in the second, more botany and zoology, a subject then called natural history and known in undergraduate parlance as "Smellie," after the author of the text generally used in the colleges. In the third year chemistry, physics and astronomy supplied hearty fare. In the last, only geology was required. Is it just coincidence that geology was also required in the senior year at Amherst, Williams, Dartmouth and Bowdoin? The title of one of Professor Hitchcock's books may provide a clue: *Religion of Geology and Its Connected Sciences.*

We may ask how the work in science at Mount Holyoke could have been as good as it seems to have been when so many of the teachers were young and untrained. A partial explanation lies, surprisingly enough, in the arrangement of the school year which, though it followed in most ways that of the colleges, differed in one fortunate respect. Except for Dartmouth's experiment with four terms, the school year was divided into three terms, fall, winter and summer, graduation coming sometime in July, at the end of the summer term. The fall term began variously from late August to Mount Holyoke's second or third week in September, but in all the schools it ended just before that most important New England holiday, Thanksgiving. The fortunate difference in calendar arrangement that so greatly benefited Mount Holyoke was the greater length of the winter vacation in the men's colleges, six to eight weeks between Thanksgiving and the beginning of the winter term as compared with Mount Holyoke's two weeks. This long vacation, designed to give needy students a chance to earn part of their expenses by teaching the winter session in country schools, was a boon to Mount Holyoke, for during it, college professors were available for lecturing. In Sarah Dickey's first year, we recall, a Bowdoin professor came down at this time to spend three weeks at Mount Holyoke, living in the Seminary and giving two lectures daily. Among those who came for shorter or longer periods at Christmas or at other times during Sarah Dickey's four years were men from Amherst, Williams, Yale, Dartmouth and Bowdoin.

It is easy to imagine what it meant to the teachers, to have the opportunity to know these scholars, to talk over the work with them and absorb new ideas. For the younger ones it amounted almost to a sort of teacher-training experience. The presence of these scholars explains also the use in the Seminary of some very up-to-date material; for example, a manual of inorganic chemistry published in the spring of 1866 was used at Mount Holyoke in the fall of that same year. Some of the men came year after year. Professor Paul Chadbourne of Williams, later its president, lectured on chemistry at Mount Holyoke for twelve years. In Sarah Dickey's third year Professor Ebenezer Snell of Amherst, who for sixteen years had lectured at Mount Holyoke on natural philosophy, as physics was then called, and had helped to buy and install necessary equipment for the course, was succeeded there by a young Dartmouth professor, Charles A. Young, who became known later as Princeton's distinguished astronomer. For almost thirty years he was lecturer and good friend to Mount Holyoke. So great was his contribution that in 1880 he was made a Mount Holyoke trustee. These many lecturers supplemented seminary work chiefly in the sciences, history, philosophy and religion. They kept both teachers and students on their academic toes and were in part responsible for the reputation for high standards that the Seminary had.

That reputation was due also to two innovations introduced some thirty years earlier by Mary Lyon, the two-course plan and the topical recitation. For their source she was probably indebted to Rev. Joseph Emerson, whose school for young teachers at Byfield, Massachusetts she had attended in 1821. In her own later teaching she was able to try out some of his original ideas, and by the time Mount Holyoke opened in 1837 her considerable experience as a successful teacher had convinced her that a few subjects studied intensively over a shorter period of time produced better results than more subjects spread over a longer period. Therefore at Mount Holyoke Seminary usually only two subjects were taken at a time and a minimum of two hours of preparation was required for each class hour; in the colleges examined four, five, and even six courses were required in each term. Most of these courses were recitation courses and, like those at Mount Holyoke, based on the study of a given textbook. Occasional supplementary lectures are sometimes mentioned in the college catalogues.

At Mount Holyoke, in part perhaps to compensate for inexperienced teachers and certainly because Mary Lyon considered the method a sound one, she had introduced a practice of recitation by topic that was rather special. The instructor, having picked out a series of topics from the material assigned for the day, would then in class call on each student to discuss one of them. The student could not do this unless she had really understood the text, for she had to select from it and organize what was needed for the given topic and then present it in her own words. No memorized repetition of the text was accepted; total recall was frowned upon. A former student of Mary Lyon, writing about her Mount Holyoke days, has this to say:

I believe that the system of recitation by topics, initiated by Miss Lyon, has never been surpassed by any of the so-called 'methods' of the present. She used to say, "Commence your topics with a brief sentence.

Let none of your periods be long. Avoid the use of the copulative conjunction *and*. State your ideas and facts clearly and consecutively, not in the words of the book but in your own best English. Aim to speak smoothly, not with hitches and jerks. Stop when you have done."

Presumably the good sense of these directions was passed down to later generations. This close textbook study was supplemented by reading in the carefully chosen but much too small library, by the occasional lecturer and in some of the sciences by field trips. Constant reviewing was also part of the system. A review of the previous lesson began each recitation period and a review of all the work of the previous week began the work of each succeeding week.

One would like to know how with only four recitation days a week and only two subjects taken at a time, with the time-consuming process of constant reviewing and the finished topical recitation, all the required subjects could possibly have been fitted into four years. To be sure, the year was forty weeks long, the terms eleven, fourteen, and fifteen weeks respectively, and the courses, term courses. (In the colleges there was a fair number of two-term courses, roughly the equivalent in time of the present-day year course.) But even so, it seems clear that at the Seminary there must have been some half-term subjects. Such brief and intensive courses could not have covered as much ground as the same courses spread over more time as they were in the colleges. It is possible, though, that what was learned was learned more thoroughly. Certainly the students' minds were well disciplined and what went into them was sound and durable.

Not all the academic work was handled by means of the term course. In the four colleges and at the Seminary there was one subject that ran continuously through every term in every year for all four years. In the colleges it was something called Declamation; at Mount Holyoke it was English composition. The classical ideal of the trained public speaker still flourished in the colleges, reinforced from their beginning by the purpose for which the colleges had been founded — to provide a trained ministry for pulpits in New England and elsewhere. Two of the colleges set aside a special day of the week for this training in composing and delivering speeches. All included supporting courses such as rhetoric and elocution. Amherst freshmen had special work on English definitions, English synonyms, English sentences, spelling and pronunciation, the last two subjects glamorized by their Greek names, orthography and orthoepy.

Mount Holyoke in the 1860's had no need to prepare her students for public speaking, their only opportunity being that of the topical recitation at the final examinations in July open to the public. Women were not welcome on public platforms. But the written word was another matter. Every student every week throughout her four years wrote a composition on which she was expected to spend a minimum of four hours. Saturday, the day assigned to this work and known as composition day, was divided between non-academic activities such as care of rooms and clothes — there was a weekly wardrobe inspection — and the production of an original composition. Looking at some of the old compositions deposited in the Mount Holyoke archives, one observes a considerable gamut in the subjects chosen and the time spent on them. The production time, always given at the end, ranges from two-and-a-half hours to nine. The subjects vary even more and seem to indicate that the students chose their own. There is a sober-face, tongue-in-cheek treatise on "Scouring Knives as Practiced at Mt. Holyoke Female Seminary" that amusingly reveals the super-thoroughness of seminary ways. Then there is that paper on Mount Holyoke's need for a gymnasium which, read at commencement, started a fund for the building. There are also stiff conventional little essays on subjects such as Youth, Religion, Nature. Spontaneity marks still others. One student who had already spent seven hours on a workmanlike report of an anti-feminist lecture at the village church ends abruptly with the words, "I haven't time to remember any more." For Sarah Dickey, who had had little work of this sort and who found, she tells us, writing difficult, Saturdays gave her training that she needed and later put to good use.

Equally serviceable to her and far more congenial was the

four-year Bible requirement which gave her a firm foundation for her own later work in the subject. The intensive study of certain books from the Old and New Testament was supplemented by a term course on a book about the Bible. While the colleges had no regular courses called Bible, the students had the advantage of reading some of the New Testament in the original Greek; at Bowdoin, where Hebrew was given in the last two terms of senior year, they tried their hand at some simple Old Testament passages. At Williams, under Mark Hopkins who was president at the time, seniors studied every Saturday morning not the Bible but a work on the catechism, "thus connecting with the truths of philosophy and of Natural Theology those of Revealed Religion." Though in the Amherst catalogue we read of required daily Bible study throughout the four years, it is not listed with the academic work but with matters dealing with the religious life of the students, required morning and evening prayers, for example, and the regular Thursday evening religious lecture by the president of Amherst to which the students were "invited." Church attendance was required at all the colleges and at the Seminary. The Williams catalogue is very specific:

Punctual attendance is required at Church, and at morning and evening Prayers, as on other College exercises. A record is kept of all delinquencies in these duties, and, with an account of the general deportment of each student, is sent to his parents or guardian.

Nor was there anything peculiar to Mount Holyoke about the highly charged religious atmosphere, the concern for the "salvation" of souls, the pressure on the unconverted. Actually Dr. Kirk, eminent Boston divine and for many years chairman of Mount Holyoke's Board of Trustees, thought the Seminary rather deficient in this respect and came himself to deal with those who had "no hope." So did trustee Henry Durant who was not a clergyman but a businessman. Evangelism was in the air.

As far as Sarah Dickey was concerned, all this emphasis on religion was welcome after her religiously starved childhood. But it added nothing to the depth and quality of her faith.

That had been established by her own church. The contribution she received from the religious life of the Seminary was of a different order. Heretofore she had known only her own church to which she was always deeply devoted. At Mount Holyoke she came to know young women belonging to different Protestant denominations. She became aware of the underlying unity that bound the various sects represented there. They all worshiped in their different ways one God. Perhaps this explains why she never proselytized for her own denomination even after she became an ordained minister. She accepted and encouraged already established religious affiliations.

This unscheduled part Mount Holyoke played in Sarah Dickey's religious education is really a phase of what we might call education by association, an education experienced by all students as a result of being in a community made up of people from various backgrounds. During Sarah Dickey's four years she was with young women from twenty-two states and seven foreign countries. The South was well represented as was also a section of the Middle West, but there was no one from farther west than Minnesota and Iowa. Excepting the girls from Canada, the students from foreign countries were most of them daughters of missionaries, many of them born overseas. In the Seminary, the geographical spread was slightly larger than that in the four colleges for men. So soon after the Civil War young Southerners did not care to enroll in a "Yankee" college. The record of the straw vote cast at Mount Holyoke for President of the United States in the November 1868 election shows that the girls from the South voted with the South for Seymour.

Another aspect of this education by association was the opportunity Sarah Dickey had to know and be known by some of the men who were directing home and foreign missions. Dr. Clark of the American Missionary Association and a newly appointed trustee of Mount Holyoke, often visited the Seminary and knew Sarah Dickey. Years later he wrote an appreciative testimonial for her. Visitors from Presbyterian and Baptist mission boards are also mentioned in the *Seminary Journal*. And we read of teachers attending the women's section of mission board meetings in Pittsfield, Buffalo, Boston and New York who on their return gave the seminary family full reports. The students were well informed about what was going on in the religious world.

They learned of it also from missionary visitors. No term was without its quota. During Sarah Dickey's years she could have heard firsthand accounts of China, India, Ceylon, Turkey, Persia, Palestine, Polynesia and Africa. One program, especially enjoyed, was that by two Williams College undergraduates, sons of missionaries in Persia and Palestine respectively. They dressed in costume, sang native songs, gave the Mohammedan call for prayer and generally delighted their audience. The girls who had come from Mohammedan countries pronounced their portrayal accurate.

Not all the talks were in missionary context. A series of lectures on conditions, political and social, in the then present-day Italy, Spain, and Brazil was given in the church under Seminary auspices for both Seminary and village. Returned travelers told of their experiences. We read of various teachers spending a year or half a year or even just a summer in Europe and returning with photographs, books and other material for the Seminary and always with interesting things to tell the students. Seminary students of the time were well inoculated against provincialism.

They also knew about and were proud of their own inheritance from the immediate past. Almost every year someone turned up who had known Mary Lyon and who brought her to life for them. In Sarah Dickey's senior year a committee of twenty-five state legislators arrived in South Hadley on official business and took time off to visit the school of which they had recently heard so much. They were shown all over the Seminary and royally entertained at tea. In the group was an old friend of Mary Lyon who had accompanied her on some of her money-raising expeditions in the hill towns of Berkshire county. He told stories of her persuasive power — some who seemed scarcely able to give ten dollars readily gave a hundred. When the time came for Sarah Dickey to raise money for her school, how heartening must have been the memory of Mary Lyon's exploits!

Sarah Dickey's senior year was memorable in other ways. It was the first year of the steam heat, greatly appreciated in spite of unpredictable, ominous clankings that interrupted recitations and prayer meetings alike. The November election aroused enormous interest, and in March during the time Ulysses S. Grant took his oath of office every activity in the Seminary was suspended so that all might pray for his wise guidance of the troubled country. This was also the year when the Seminary was wakened at midnight by the cry of fire. The house and barn adjacent on the north were ablaze. Everyone got out in record time to form a bucket brigade that saved some neighboring buildings. Another local event of the year, an important one for Mount Holyoke, was breaking ground on the fifteenth of June for the fireproof library that would house Mrs. Durant's gift of ten thousand dollars' worth of books.

But for Sarah Dickey, the most important event of her senior year was making the decision she had uneasily put off from year to year ever since her first month at Mount Holyoke when she heard the voice telling her she should build a school in the South for colored girls like the one she had just entered, an idea she had been unwilling to accept as coming from God, yet half believing it. She tells us about her final decision in the *Dew of Hermon* account quoted from earlier. After explaining that although she felt more drawn to missionary work in Africa, the thought of work in the South would not leave her, she wrote:

So, as our last fast day drew on in April, I made up my mind that I should settle that question that day. I prayed about it all day until about four o'clock in the afternoon, receiving no reply whatever. Then as I sat in my room I said, "Lord, I have prayed over this all day, and I feel just as I have felt all these years; I prefer to go to Africa, but a voice seems to say I must do that work in the South. Now," I said: "Lord, how shall I decide?" And then the voice spoke and said: "Go and tell Miss Ward all about it, and let whatever she says be the decision." I arose immediately and went to Miss Ward's room and told her all that was in my heart on this subject, and when I had finished she sat quiet for a moment and then said, "Well, Sarah if you think of doing the work you say you do if you remain in America, I think you would better remain in America." That settled it. And when I graduated the 15th of the next July, 1869, and then looked back and traced the hand of God as He led me through all the little things and big things of those four years, I said, "God could never ask me to do anything that I should fear to undertake."

From that moment she went steadily, patiently, unswervingly forward in spite of what appeared to be insuperable difficulties. Had she chosen the foreign mission field, the way would have been cleared for her — all arrangements made by the Mission Board and a regular stipend assured. As it was, she must carve out her way unaided.

She was already in debt. Every step of her last three years had been a financial struggle. No further windfall like that early sixty dollars came her way. We know very little about how she managed. We have a few names of people who helped her — the Goldthwaits, Mrs. Byron Smith and the Durants. We know that at one point she was reduced to selling two of her dresses and her Saratoga trunk. We know that during her second summer she made a good thing out of house-to-house canvassing for Smith's *Dictionary of the Bible,* a classic in the field. And we know that in the end she had to borrow money from the Seminary in order to graduate. That is all our positive knowledge, although the three names above give ground for some probable guesses. The Goldthwaits lived on a farm northeast of the Seminary. Mr. Goldthwait, with his partner Mr. Spooner, supplied the school with pork, beef, sausage and chicken during Sarah Dickey's first two years. Mrs. Goldthwait boarded students in their big farmhouse during the two short vacations of the year. It was a friendly household, as we learn from a student's letter telling of an invitation for Christmas dinner received by the seventeen who had vacationed there. Mr. Goldthwait drove them back and forth in his big sleigh and Mrs. Goldthwait cooked a memorable meal. All had a jolly time. After the end of Sarah Dickey's second year we hear no more of the Goldthwaits. They probably moved west to better farming land, as they had talked of doing. But during those first two years Sarah Dickey probably spent the short vacations with them, earning her room and board by helping with the housework.

The Byron Smiths had a home in the village as well as a farm on the outskirts. Mrs. Smith, Nancy Dwight before her marriage, and Byron Smith, son of Erastus Smith, Mary Lyon's good friend, both came from well-to-do South Hadley families. Byron Smith, like his father before him, marshaled the Anniversary Day procession from the Seminary to the church where the graduation exercises were held. Perhaps Mrs. Smith took Sarah Dickey in for the short vacations after the Goldthwaits left, doubtless helping her in other ways.

The aid the Durants gave came in Sarah Dickey's last two years. After Mr. Durant had been appointed a Mount Holyoke trustee in 1867, he and his wife were often at the Seminary, once spending an entire week there. They would have known Sarah Dickey personally. It seems likely that their help would have been financial. She was working hard with no margin of time in which she could earn the extra money she needed. We are told by one of the teachers that she was thin and anxious looking. How could she be otherwise? Yet she always thought of these years of gruelling work with the warmest affection. They had brought her all she had longed for — and more.

As Sarah Dickey approached the end of her Mount Holyoke years, her thoughts were directed to her immediate future in a special way. A man from Athens, Georgia, Col. C. G. Baylor, was to be the Anniversary Day speaker for her class. He had received permission from the seminary teachers to enlist the interest of the class in a certain project of his, a Mary Lyon Seminary for Negro girls in Mississippi. He had already produced a printed prospectus, the title page of which reads, *The Mary Lyon Female Seminary and Educational Home of Mississippi founded under the Auspices of the American Missionary Association on the plan of the Mt. Holyoke Female Seminary at South Hadley, Mass.* Colonel Baylor was already known to the students and liked by them. Dr. Kirk, chairman of Mount Holyoke's Board of Trustees and an officer of the American

Missionary Association, had brought him to visit the Seminary the previous fall. The Colonel had been immensely impressed by the domestic work system, so foreign to Southern custom. A man of lively imagination, he was at once convinced that for rebuilding his native Southland, the do-it-yourself idea involved in such a system could work wonders. He spoke one morning in seminary hall, telling of his prewar days when he had been a prosperous slaveholder, living a life of idle ease. After the war he found himself, like so many others, a poor man, stripped of all he had, but, unlike most of the others, not filled with hate. He had undergone a change of heart and wanted to give his life to building a better South. The part of women in such work, he felt, was all-important, a theme on which he enlarged. He wanted a school established in his home town of Athens for young white ladies on the model of Mount Holyoke. It is the last we hear of that idea; in the intervening nine months he had become interested in the work of the American Missionary Association and had turned his attention to the pitiable condition of the freedmen.

Only a few days after his visit the interest of Mount Holyoke students had been turned in that same direction by no less a person than General Howard, head of the Freedmen's Bureau, then in its last year. General Howard had talked about the great need for work among the freedmen and the many hardships the workers would have to face. As a result of his talk and others, Seminary interest in the plight of the freedmen was keen.

But to return to Colonel Baylor, a letter he addressed to the head of the American Missionary Association reads:

I believe by the Grace of God I have found the work I am to do in connection with your established interests. It is reflected in the simple idea that there must be reared up out of the native material of the South, a standard of Christian womanhood to be at once a standard, a stimulant and example to the women of the African Race. The *ideal* is a Mount Holyoke in each Southern state for the colored girls who are to become the regenerated and regenerating mothers of their race, teachers, missionaries and companions of those who fight the battle of African Christian civilization on the continent of America.

In another letter he asked to have made out for him "a specific and detailed statement of the schools in the South upon which we can graft our Mt. Holyokes."

We know what he said at Sarah Dickey's graduation, although, unlike most of the speeches given on Anniversary Day, it was never printed. In a letter to an official of the American Missionary Association he said that with the permission of the teachers at Mount Holyoke, he had placed the founding of a Mary Lyon Seminary in Mississippi under the direct patronage of the graduating class and had told them that as soon as the Association gave permission they could prepare an appeal for funds to be sent to all Mount Holyoke alumnae. Evidently he had heard of the successful steam-heat letters but did not know that the Association had no official connection with Mount Holyoke. After picturing what he called the almost sub-animal conditions in which many freedmen were living, he outlined his plans for the Mary Lyon schools in the South and proceeded to the Mississippi one which the class of 1869 was to take under its wing. Its location was practically assured, he said, for the American Missionary Association had just bought a plantation near Jackson, where it could be opened as soon as the needed $10,000 was subscribed.

Unfortunately the Colonel proved to be no money raiser. The American Missionary Association, which had been employing him as a sort of agent, found him increasingly hard to work with. The following month his business relations with it came to an end, though not his friendship with some of its members. The correspondence shows how difficult the practical-minded Northerners had found it to work with this idealistic, silver-tongued Southerner. They recognized his integrity and dedication, but they distrusted his judgment, lack of experience, and the multiplicity of his projects. The American Missionary Association, later in 1869, opened a school on the plantation originally assigned to the Mary Lyon Seminary. In 1871 it was chartered as Tougaloo University, a name that was changed in 1916 to Tougaloo College. No word has come down of any Mary Lyon Seminary.

But during Sarah Dickey's last term the project was in its hey-day. It came before the Mount Holyoke teachers who, as we have seen, regarded it with favor. What part had Sarah Dickey in all this? She was the one person who knew the Mississippi freedmen at first hand and had finally dedicated her life to their cause. It is hard to believe that Miss Ward, who was an associate principal at the time, did not in some way connect her with Colonel Baylor and the Mississippi Mary Lyon Seminary, but if so, no record remains. Indeed, as far as Mount Holyoke goes, except for an account in the *Seminary Journal* of the Colonel's visit in the fall and his name on the Anniversary Day program, he and his Mary Lyon seminaries might never have been. Yet for a time it may have seemed to Sarah Dickey that her immediate future was assured. That she does not mention the matter causes no surprise. She never wasted time or thought on any water that had gone over the dam.

If she had entertained such a prospect, it was by no means the only thing on her mind. The end of a school year, always an exhausting time, was especially so for those graduating at Mount Holyoke during seminary days because final examinations were oral, public, and part of the commencement festivities. The pressure such an arrangement put on the members of the senior class is easy to imagine. However, before all this pressure began mounting, the class of 1869 had been busy with its own affairs. In May its members composed and adopted a constitution, the preamble of which reads:

We, the Class of '69 of Mt. Holyoke Seminary, in order to form a more perfect union, to provide for the transaction of business and to devise means of communication between the members of the class after our separation do ordain and establish this constitution by which we pledge ourselves to be governed.

The "means of communication" provided for was the publication of a class letter to which each member was expected to contribute. Of the seven letters published at widely varying intervals during Sarah Dickey's lifetime — the last was in 1901 — she contributed to only three. Yet receiving these letters meant a great deal to her. She grieved at not having received the first (1870) although she had not contributed to it. Many years later (1901) she wrote that the news there was to be another class letter "acted quite as a panacea to my returning strength after a very short but very severe attack of illness." She wanted to know "the whereabouts and welfare of the different members of the class."

Another matter taken care of by the constitution was the appointment of two poets and four prophets who were to produce their wares for '69's Class Day. Class Day was an important occasion. It came some three weeks before graduation and was a strictly private affair. Members of the graduating class were excused from all appointments on that day and had their dinner together in one of the parlors. The prophecies and poems were read and an original song was sung with gusto to the rattling of spoons. Each member of the class was toasted in turn. Sarah Dickey's toast was "May she find her accustomed seat in a Southern School and may dusky faces lighten with pleasure at her approach." The word "accustomed" gives evidence that Sarah Dickey had talked with her classmates about her Vicksburg experiences and also about what she was planning to do. Miss Ward, an associate principal and favorite teacher, perhaps an honorary member of the class, provided a more serious note at the end in her toast to the class.

> Bright be the skies above you,
> Dear daughters of our home
> And smooth the path before you
> Wherever you may roam.
> And when, all labors ended,
> To reach life's setting sun,
> To highest heaven ascended,
> May each hear Christ's "Well done."

Class Day was certainly more enjoyed than commencement week itself. The days of public examination must have been a considerable strain for the participants, though the guests found them enjoyable. We are fortunate in having a detailed account of '69's last days written for the *Springfield Republican* by a reporter who obviously liked his assignment and was determined to show how thorough and judicious, lively and descriptive he could be. Perhaps he himself had recently graduated from college; on internal evidence he would appear to have been young. He begins by congratulating Mount Holyoke for not having "the inevitable baccalaureate on Sunday."

Like good Christians they [the students] begin the labors and delights of graduation on Monday; and these consist chiefly in examinations, music, and composition reading. Visitors are spared the interminable oratory and speech-making which make this season at a masculine educational institution such a dreadful ordeal to pass. . . . Searching public examinations in philosophy, science, mathematics, and the languages, relieved by occasional reading of essays and instrumental and vocal music, occupied the whole of Monday [actually they did not begin till three o'clock Monday afternoon]. Tuesday and Wednesday, and this morning [Thursday] the senior class finished this harassing work by a recitation in Wayland's *Moral Science* in the public hall of the seminary building. The class, 38 in number, were arranged in double file across the middle of the hall, which was crowded with relatives and friends and the curious in general. When the recitation began one of the files arose and responded as each was called upon, and then gave way to the other. Each girl was dressed in white, with a broad blue sash over her shoulder, and vigorously fluttered a natty little fan, while the cross-questioning went on. The general effect of that row of white-clad maidens, each of whom at the length of the hall looked the counterpart of the other, and all intently bent on keeping cool if the fans could do it, was rather funny, but this soon gave place to more respectful feelings, when the recitation began. A name was called and some abstruse and knotty ethical question propounded. Then, with most astonishing promptness, the topic was taken up and in a neat, crisp little speech of two or three minutes developed, expounded, finished. Each member of the class was called upon and, almost without an exception, each showed the same surprising readiness. This brilliancy in reciting is due in large measure, of course, to a girl's naturally quick and retentive memory; yet we fancy few college students have a clearer comprehension of these subjects at the end of senior year than these girls displayed, today. At all events they do not show that they have.

A short recess followed the close of this exercise . . . till the marshal's sharp rap restored order again, and a selection by Mendelssohn by a chorus of girls was announced. The singing of this chorus was very fine, and showed that its members had had excellent training. The higher notes were all clear and full, but the complete effect of the piece was lost from lack of bass. There was no ground tone on which the harmony could be built. In this little thing, even, one felt how in-effectual one sex is without its complement in the other.

Next was the reading of five compositions by members of the gradu-ating class. These essays were, with one exception, picturesque and rhetorical in style and had in them more of sentiment than of thought. ... The one exception was a review of Auerbach's novel, *On the Heights,* in which the thought and purpose of the book were acutely analyzed, and the author's power and position as a thinker defined. The writer showed much knowledge of the systems of Hegel and Plato,— for here they wax not pale at such philosophic draughts. As a piece of purely literary criticism it was not, perhaps, unusual, but as a philosophic estimate of a great work it was remarkable for a young woman.

When all these compositions had been read and the parting song sung by the class, the procession . . . marched to the village church.

The reporter tells at some length of Colonel Baylor's address, which did not especially impress him. He thought it dealt with politics more than necessary and "in style was suggestive of con-vention halls and platforms." At its close, he continues:

Rev. Edward N. Kirk of Boston, president of the trustees, said the fare-well words to the senior class, and tender and wise words they were. It was only a little speech, but it was full of pathos, of fatherly admoni-tion, of encouragement, of warning, of hope. Then the diplomas were distributed among the class. . . .

The account goes on for another column or so. We are told of the procession back from the church, of the meal that was served to the guests by the pretty hostesses, a meal that is vari-ously called by the enthusiastic reporter a collation, spread, and dinner. In the afternoon the guests were taken over the build-ings and grounds, the mysteries of the domestic work system explained and the foundations for the fireproof library in-spected. Then the reporter had to return to Springfield to get his copious copy ready for the morning paper. At the end of his account of the day, he wrote "This evening [July 15, 1869] a reception will be given by the members of the senior class to their friends and invited guests, and then the thirty-second anniversary of Mount Holyoke Seminary will be over."

It is good to have this vivid picture of the academic and social activities that climaxed Sarah Dickey's student days at Mount Holyoke. We can almost see her on that hot July day marching back from the church in her white dress, doubtless her own handiwork, a wide sash draped from shoulder to waist, its blue matching the blue of her eyes, with her hard-won diploma in her hand. Over-modest, even self-depreciatory, as a classmate has described her, she could scarcely have been unaware of her achievement. Her class had numbered one hundred when it entered Mount Holyoke. For Sarah Dickey to be one of the thirty-eight to graduate was in itself a triumph. The "further education" she had so painfully struggled to get was now hers. It had fed her mind and given her a sense of worlds before unknown to her. At the same time her seminary years had given her what she never had before, a sense of "home" and of "belonging." She had made friends among both teachers and classmates whose interest and friendship continued throughout her life. And she had learned methods of organization that would serve her well in the work that she was sure the Lord intended her to do. Her days of preparation were over.

4.   Return to Mississippi

For Sarah Dickey, as for most of us, peak moments —
moments of triumph, of confidence, of ecstasy — are followed
by their opposites — periods of frustration, of uncertainty, of
desolation. She was alone, her classmates scattered far and
wide to their homes, most of them with plans for the future.
Grief over her father's death was still fresh upon her. In his
blundering way he had tried to do what he could for her. She
had looked forward to a visit with him at the end of her seminary course; her diploma would have pleased him. Physically
she was exhausted from the struggle of the four years just
ended. One of her teachers described her as "a spare figure,
looking tired and overwrought, but a faithful worker and
diligent student."

In debt for her education, she was faced by two conflicting
necessities — that of paying off her indebtedness and that of
obeying the voice that had told her to build a school in the
South like Mount Holyoke. In what way should she go about
such difficult and divergent tasks? She needed help in deciding
how to begin and she needed a place where she could rest and
gain strength for what she must do. The one member of her
family who could supply these needs was the married sister to
whom she had gone on her return from Vicksburg. We know
her, strangely enough, only as Mrs. Mather, nor do we know
the given name of any other member of Sarah Dickey's family.

To earn money for the journey to her sister was consequently
a first objective. So she found work as she had done on the three
previous summers, and as soon as she had earned the needed
sum, she started on the long trip west, probably in September.

This time she provided herself with food for the almost three days of day coach travel. She stopped off at Dayton, Ohio, to see her relatives and friends there and to worship in what she now regarded as her church home, the Dayton First Church of the United Brethren in Christ. During those early years of study and teaching in the general Dayton area, she had grown attached to this church and its people. That is why in 1864, while she was in Vicksburg, she had her membership transferred from Lewisburg to Dayton. Though she never again lived near Dayton, she always kept in touch with that center of United Brethren work. More than once the church or some organization in it loaned her money, and various church members were generous supporters of her later work. On her many later trips North she never failed to stop in Dayton, where she always drew strength from the warm fellowship.

Now, refreshed by that fellowship, she continued her journey west. While she was at Mount Holyoke the Mathers had moved from Richmond, Indiana, to Winona, Wisconsin, a small town on the western border of the state just across the Mississippi River from the better known Winona, Minnesota. Sarah Dickey liked the idea of being so near the river that had carried her down to Vicksburg and could take her that way again should any position materialize for her.

Something did materialize for her; both Vicksburg and Mount Holyoke played a part. Two Mount Holyoke trustees were also officers of the American Missionary Association. This organization (referred to in this text as the A.M.A.), founded in 1846 with one of its main objectives the abolition of caste, had done much of its early work in Siam, the Sandwich Islands, Jamaica and in North America among Eskimos, American Indians, and American Orientals. With the signing of the Emancipation Proclamation it moved into the South, focusing its efforts on educational work for the freedmen. At one time it had charge over 250 schools as well as the seven colleges that today merit a place on the list of colleges helped by the United Negro College Fund. The schools, most of them elementary, were to serve as stopgaps until such time as individual counties and towns in the South were able and willing to take over full responsibility for adequate Negro elementary and secondary education. In its early work in the South the A.M.A. cooperated with the Freedmen's Bureau. Sarah Dickey's old friend, Chaplain Warren, at first the Bureau's superintendent of Negro education for Mississippi, had been succeeded by Captain Henry R. Pease, another of the Bureau's agents. Captain Pease seems to have been the one who suggested Sarah Dickey's name to the officers of the A.M.A. Whether he knew her personally or only through Dr. Warren is not clear. In any case, through him Sarah Dickey's excellent work in Vicksburg became known to the A.M.A. officials who already knew her good record at Mount Holyoke.

Thus it was no accident that while Sarah Dickey was with her sister an opportunity such as she had longed for came almost within reach. A Boston woman, Miss H. C. Bullard, in charge of an A.M.A. school in Raymond, Mississippi, needed assistance. The A.M.A. felt it could pay a helper but not that helper's traveling expenses. If Miss Dickey could get herself to Raymond the position was hers.

Here was exactly the work she wanted, apparently just out of reach. Only apparently, however; her prayers that a way might open were answered. Mrs. Mather, in full sympathy with her sister, had talked to her friends in the local Congregational church about what her sister hoped to do. These church ladies, good Congregationalists, knew of the A.M.A.'s work in the South which was largely under Congregational management. Here was Mrs. Mather's sister, clearly a competent, experienced person, who offered them an opportunity to have a part in the good work. No wonder they took fire! It was a big task for them. The church was small, their means slight and the time short. Yet by December they had the needed amount and Sarah Dickey once more embarked on a river boat for Vicksburg.

Was the journey down the Mississippi full of memories of that adventuresome earlier trip? Probably not; Sarah Dickey's nature was to look forward, not backward. Her thoughts were more likely to have been centered on means for realizing her dream. She was going back to Mississippi — that was a first step. She would be receiving a salary, a small one to be sure, but enough to make some saving possible with which to reduce her debt — that was at least the beginning of a second step. Once at Vicksburg she would seek out people who could brief her on the changes during her absence, people who might also help her in the future. Indeed a better place than Vicksburg for catching up on all that concerned the Mississippi Negro could not have been found. Not only had the activities of the Freedman's Bureau and those of the military government been centered there, but Vicksburg Negroes were a leading group in the state. They had sent a strongly worded request to Congress urging that body to refuse Mississippi readmission to the Union until it gave the vote and other civil rights to the Negro. The majority in Congress were already in accord, but the initiative shown confirmed their belief in the Negro.

Sarah Dickey landed at Vicksburg a little after the middle of December as she had done just six years earlier. But what a different Vicksburg it was! Buildings had been repaired and order restored. The streets were no longer thronged with Negro refugees. The A.M.A. agent who met her boat explained that all jobless Negroes had been evicted from the city as a health measure. They had died like flies in the cholera epidemic of 1866; tuberculosis, to which they were especially susceptible, was taking its toll. More than a thousand had already died in the Vicksburg area alone. Crowded and unsanitary living conditions continued to breed disease throughout the state. Those few who had got a start that seemed to promise independence had been ruined by the crop failures of '66 and '67. The plight of the great mass of Mississippi Negroes was painfully evident, and Sarah Dickey, listening intently to all she was told by the agent and others, noted what she must stress when the school she had come to build took shape.

She was challenged, too, by the belief of many white citizens that the Negro could not long survive outside the protective care of slavery. They pointed for confirmation to the appalling mortality figures among Negroes since they had been freed. It was officially said that half the Negro population of the state had already died, and it was generally believed that the rest must follow. Editorials in the chief Mississippi papers had commented rather happily on the prospect. The Negro was a feckless child unable to care for himself. It was just a matter of patience for a while until, like the dodo, he became extinct. A highly respected preacher prophesied that by January 1, 1920 "the colored population in the South will scarcely be counted. . . ." One writer said that the child was already born who would see the last Negro in Mississippi.

Sarah Dickey was saddened as well as challenged by these predictions. They showed so little sympathy with and understanding of the Negro. She had hoped that in the first years of his freedom something would have been done to prepare him for his new responsibilities. Instead the gap between the races seemed even wider and deeper than before. When she asked why, she was told about a piece of legislation enacted soon after she had left. Known as the Black Code, it was a misguided attempt to shore up the collapsing economy of a state in which all agriculture and most other work had depended on slave labor. Many ex-slaves were disinclined to work for their former masters or indeed to work at all. The labor situation was desperate. So in the fall of 1865 the legislature had passed laws that were practically caste laws since they did not apply to the white laborer. Certain ones were so extreme, like the one denying the Negro's right to buy or rent land, that Washington took notice and nullified them. But in some sections of the state little attention was paid to the nullification and the Negro's lot worsened. Though the better element in the state was not in sympathy with the more drastic parts of the code, the harm was done. For the Northern liberal it was proof that the Southerner had no intention of treating the Negro with justice. For the Negro it further widened the breach between him and his former master.

One article in the Code made labor contracts by the year practically mandatory. Negroes generally were most unwilling to sign up for a whole year, in part because of a widespread belief among them that the government in Washington, the government that had given them freedom, would also give the head of every family forty acres of land and a mule, a present that would probably come at Christmas time. For three years, '65, '66, and '67, Christmas was a time of hope for the Negro and of fear for his white neighbors who thought his disappointment might result in insurrection. Citizens in some towns armed themselves against such a possibility.

Not all that Sarah Dickey learned about the people she had come to help dealt with disappointments, injustices, disasters and disease. She learned also that throughout the state small Negro churches were springing up. In slavery days there had been almost no such churches. For the most part house servants and a few others had attended Sunday service in their master's church, sitting together in a gallery or at the back in a place reserved for them. The field hands, gathered about their cabins, had given voice to their unquestioning belief and passionate longing in their spirituals. After the war some churches were willing to let the ex-slaves continue to attend services and remain members, but unwilling to allow them any voice in the affairs of the church. This unwillingness and the steadily widening rift between the races resulted in the rise of Negro churches. Their rapid growth was due in part to the work of church organizers from the North, but even more to the zeal of the Negroes themselves. The little churches they built were their very own. Possession was a new and heady experience. No sacrifice was too great to build and maintain these centers of their social and religious life. When later Sarah Dickey was arousing interest in her school and raising money for it, she found many of these churches welcoming and helpful. By far the greatest number organized by Negroes were Baptist. The lack of ecclesiastical superstructure in the Baptist church and the fact that each congregation was practically autonomous meant that groups could and did spring up all over the state.

The Methodist church built the next largest number. Of the four branches of Methodists represented in Mississippi, the African Methodist Episcopal church was the most active, largely because of the work of Rev. T. W. Stringer, a Negro originally from Ohio now presiding elder in the church at Vicksburg. A born organizer, he traveled about the state leaving a trail of churches behind him. He had settled in Vicksburg early in 1865 and as Sarah Dickey did not leave until August, she may have met him then; but whether she knew him personally or not, she would have heard about him because of his political as well as his church-organizing activities. He was a prime mover in setting up a Republican organization among Negroes in Vicksburg and he was able to exert some influence in the constitutional convention of 1868, derisively called the Black and Tan convention because out of the one hundred delegates sixteen were colored. Charles Caldwell, another Negro delegate active in that convention, was only a name to Sarah Dickey then. In the not-too-distant future, however, he was to play an important part in her life. The name of a third Negro was possibly known to her, Rev. Hiram Rhodes Revels. He did not figure in state politics at this time, but as presiding elder of the African Methodist Episcopal church in Natchez he was associated with the church-building work of Rev. T. W. Stringer. Later Revels was to become the first Negro senator, filling out the unexpired term of Jefferson Davis. From all accounts Revels acquitted himself well in Washington.

Stringer, Caldwell and Revels were three of the five Negroes just elected to the state senate that would soon be seated. They are interesting to us because all three became members of Sarah Dickey's first Board of Trustees when finally her school was organized. Mississippi was more fortunate than some of her neighboring states in having among her Negroes such men, men of intelligence, initiative and integrity.

Sarah Dickey heard much about that discredited "Black and Tan" constitutional convention of 1868 to which Stringer and Caldwell had been elected. Its purpose was to produce a constitution on the basis of which Mississippi could be readmitted to the Union. Congress had stipulated as minimum requirements that it must ensure the Negro's right to vote and to hold office as well as ratifying the thirteenth and fourteenth amendments to the constitution of the United States. That such re-

quirements were repugnant to Mississippi Democrats goes
without saying. And when General Ord, the military governor
of the moment, announced that Negroes not only could vote in
the election for delegates to that convention but could also act
as clerks and judges at it, the people felt openly insulted. Their
reaction to this ruling is expressed in the following extract from
an editorial of the time in the *Vicksburg Herald.*

> We hoped that this shameful humiliation would have been spared
> our people, at least until the freemen of Mississippi decide whether
> they will submit to negro equality at the ballot box or elsewhere . . . .
> we doubt not that lovers of peace throughout the country will condemn
> the order as injudicious, if not insulting to that race whom God has
> created the superior of the black man, and whom no monarch can make
> his equal.

This sense of outrage was general among Mississippi Democrats who, after all, formed the bulk of the white citizenry.
They expressed their disdain by their indifference to the election
of delegates. In Vicksburg, for instance, only eight of them
bothered to go to the polls. And when the hard-working convention finally produced a constitution and offered it to the
people for ratification, it was summarily turned down. With a
presidential election close at hand the people saw no reason for
even considering such a constitution. They firmly believed that
Horatio Seymour, the Democratic candidate, would be elected.
Then the white man's superior place in the Southern sun would
again be firmly established, and they would hear no more of
Negro "rights."

But when Republican Ulysses S. Grant was elected President
and General Adelbert Ames of Maine abolitionist stock, already
civil governor, was made military governor, there was nothing
left for Mississippi to do but make the best bargain possible
with the inevitable. The repudiated constitution was pulled
down from the shelf and shorn of a few objectionable features,
though voting and office-holding rights for the Negro had to
be retained. This revised constitution and the fourteenth and
new fifteenth amendments to our country's constitution were
ratified, and Mississippi was readmitted to the Union. Only a
month before Sarah Dickey arrived at Vicksburg elections had

been held for state officers and members of the state legislature.
Talk about the results was rife.

Certainly the native Mississippi Democrats looked with loath-
ing at the make-up of the just elected legislature. Bad as it was
to have it packed with Republicans, many of them Northerners
who had settled in Mississippi since the war, it was intolerable
that thirty-six Negroes were to be among the one hundred and
forty legislators. On the first of the next month, January 1870,
the Republican Reconstruction government would take over.
Sarah Dickey had come at a crucial moment in Mississippi
history.

Some of the Republicans with whom Sarah Dickey talked
were enthusiastic, seeing in the new government possibilities of
reform and advance. Perhaps Captain Henry R. Pease belonged
to this group. He had just been elected state superintendent of
education. Since before the war Mississippi had had no over-all
system of public education, he would have a free hand in organizing one. A second group was less optimistic but inclined to
think that anything would be better than the awkward and
confusing dual system of government under which they had
lived for five years, with a succession of military governors in
Vicksburg (three in the first year alone) and less frequently
changed civil governors in Jackson. In the third group were
those who had lived longest in the South; they were frankly
apprehensive. They feared what might happen when a government in control was alien and uncongenial to the average
citizen. From all that she had heard about what had happened
in her absence, Sarah Dickey was inclined to agree with the
third group. Things that the agent who had met her boat told
her made her realize the conditions she would meet. If he was,
as he may have been, Rev. J. P. Bardwell, an Oberlin graduate
who had been an A.M.A. agent for the Association's Negro
schools in Mississippi and who was in Vicksburg at the time,
he could have given her much firsthand information about the
increasing racial tension. He reported that the mass of people
would rather see the Negroes going to their graves than to
school and that the only reason the Southerners were interested

in training a few Negroes to teach was to get rid of the Yankee
school teachers. The more popular method of getting rid of
them, he said, was that used by the Ku Klux Klan. Its stated
aim was to clear Mississippi of all "carpet baggers." The term
covered every Northerner who had come South since the war,
whatever his purpose in coming. All were hated, though for
different reasons, perhaps the missionaries and school teachers
most because of their association with the freedmen and influence on them. While visiting a school in Grenada, a town north
of Jackson, Mr. Bardwell had been invited into the office of a
presumably reputable lawyer where he was set upon by several
men and severely beaten. Later an agent of the Freedmen's
Bureau was shot to death on a Grenada street.

These accounts and others like them did not frighten Sarah
Dickey on her own account; they simply underlined the need
for the work she had come to do, but she was fearful of what
the future might hold for the Negro. The Reconstruction government would be friendly to him, but what of the people at
large? Though the laws of the Black Code had been repealed,
men's minds and hearts remained unchanged.

Well caught up on Mississippi politics, people and problems,
Sarah Dickey took the train for Jackson; from there she went
southwest to Raymond. The journey to Jackson was through
country laid waste by Union troops, and not by them only,
but by Confederate troops as well, anxious to leave nothing
that might aid the oncoming opposing force. Yet now, five
years later, as she scanned the countryside from the car window,
she saw almost no visible sign of those dreadful days. The
scars, however, as she knew, were deep in men's hearts; resent-
ment smouldered dangerously. She could understand that it
must be so. Her warm human sympathy enabled her to see
things from another's point of view while holding firmly to
her own. This ability was one of the things that in the end won
for her the respect of her Southern neighbors. But that time
was still far off.

On her way to Jackson she passed through Clinton, the
town, though she did not know it, where her dream was to be

realized and her life lived. At Jackson she changed for the last fifteen miles of her journey. Raymond, her destination,. was and is a town of some importance as seat of Hinds County, a large county including Jackson and Clinton.

We get an idea of Raymond, Miss Bullard and the school where Sarah Dickey was to teach from some letters Miss Bullard wrote to the general field agent of the A.M.A. and from a few official monthly reports of the school, kept in the A.M.A. archives at Fisk University. It is a rather different picture from that suggested by Sarah Dickey's glorified memory of her happy year there. As compared to conditions in war-time Vicksburg, Raymond must have seemed an orderly place to Sarah Dickey, whereas Boston-bred Miss Bullard viewed it with other eyes and writes, "This is one of the worst places for its size I was ever in."

Some of the printed questions on the forms the A.M.A. teachers were expected to fill out and send monthly to the New York office tell a good deal about the work and the pupils. Among the questions were the following: How many Children and Adults, beginning with the Alphabet have you taught to read during the School Year thus far? How many have learned to write? (this was always a much smaller number). How many are more than sixteen years old? How many were free before the war? (the answer to that was always none). How many in day school? How many in night school? How many in "Sabbath School"? How many have paid tuition for the particular month concerned? The tuition money was for the teachers' support. When the field agent realized that only nineteen of the seventy-six pupils taught in Miss Bullard's first month (January, 1869) had paid any tuition and that the total was $12.00, while she was paying $25.00 a month for board, he proposed moving her to another school and giving up the one at Raymond. She replied (March 31, 1869):

I wish to do as you think best about leaving Raymond. I think however this place is an exception to the rule in respect to supporting a teacher. The children bring for their instruction, what money their parents can spare, from a few cents to a dollar each mo., and the sum of these contributions provides me with food. The Bureau pays me a salary and the rent of school building instead of half the rent as I expected. . . .

My day school is not quite as large as it was, because the larger pupils are obliged to work in the field, but when they leave the day school, they come to the night school. I have instructed about seventy eight altogether this month. . . .

I hope you will think it best for me to remain here, not that I have any enjoyment outside of my work, but it seems to me important that there should be a school here. . . . when I have a few moments to stop and think, I am very lonesome, but my work rewards me for this isolation as I go along, in seeing the vacant stare with which many of my pupils come, vanish, and a look of intelligence take its place.

Apparently it was Miss Bullard's willingness to sacrifice herself for the school (she gave up boarding out and cooked her own meals) that kept the school going for the few years of its life. After she left in 1872 with her sister who had taken Sarah Dickey's place, the school no longer appears on the A.M.A. list.

The Raymond school drew students from a wide area, some of them walking as much as three and four miles from their home and others who lived ten and twelve miles away boarding in town during the week without any supervision. Miss Bullard was greatly concerned about them and wrote the field agent. She speaks of the "numerous dram shops and other places of temptation" in Raymond. "I almost think it is my duty," she wrote, "to advise the parents not to send their children to school under these circumstances — indeed I am sorely puzzled what to do— will you advise me?" Elsewhere she had asked how to organize a temperance society.

Sometimes she was amused rather than puzzled by this so-different-from-Boston part of the world in which she found herself. She tells us that

A white Southern lady (?) who refused me a night's lodging when I first came here, now comes to my room in the afternoon, for me to show her how to perform and explain examples in fractions. She has a school for white children and has taken her first class in arithmetic as far as she had been instructed, and now she seems not to know what to do, unless it be to apply to the "Yankee school marm" for *private* instruction.

It would appear that Miss Bullard's work for the colored children was being appreciated, for she was able to write before the end for her first year,

My school is gaining favor with the white people here. Several of the best men of the town have admitted to others that it is very important there should be a school for the colored children here. The first physician of the place intends soon to start an Episcopal S.S. for the colored children.

Regrettably there are no reports in the A.M.A. archives for the year Sarah Dickey was at Raymond and only one brief business letter on a matter that did not concern her. The only mention of her name occurs in a letter Miss Bullard wrote the next year. She wanted a small portable organ and said that the year before Miss Dickey had thought she could get money for one from a friend, but her letter asking for help was never answered. Slight as this mention is, it at least shows their common interest in plans for the school. The two women could have had very little in the way of common background, but they were at one in their dedication to the cause of Negro education. We also know that the school flourished during Sarah Dickey's year there. Before she came registration was under one hundred; it started at 140 the year after she left.

Writing of her Raymond experience two years later, Sarah Dickey says,

When I landed at Raymond in January, 1870, I set out to do all the work that I could, never stopping to think of ill health or lack of means, leaving the consequences with Him who doeth all things well. I did do all that I could, and now whenever I visit Raymond I feel that I am perfectly lost in the meshes of love.

Two things here are of special interest. Her mention of ill health reminds us of her early illness when as a fourteen-year-old girl, she broke down from exposure and overwork on the farm where she had been placed after her aunt's death. Ever after she was subject to rheumatic disorders. The other is the warmth of affection that "enmeshed" her after only the single year, January to January, that she worked in the Raymond area. This is the more conspicuous because at Clinton, where she went next, she encountered distrust and animosity. She was years in winning the respect, confidence, and love that had been so easily hers in Raymond. One wonders what part Miss Bullard had in the so different climate there.

The work Sarah Dickey did during the summer vacation of her year at Raymond probably contributed to her feeling for the place and must have made many friends for her among the Negroes. She was a sort of rural missionary under the A.M.A. for the general Raymond area. She visited the women in the small cabins scattered over the countryside, trying to inculcate ideas of sanitation and child care, showing them how to "make do" with what they had. Her own experiences as child and girl growing up under almost pioneer conditions were a great help to her in this work. Negroes who had been house servants in slave days were less in need of this sort of advice and training, but most of these Negroes had been field hands, their living conditions sometimes little better than that of animals. In this work Sarah Dickey combined teaching sanitation, the alphabet, and the Gospel. It was a hard, busy and happy time, giving her a better understanding of the people to whom she had dedicated her life. The great emphasis that she later put on cleanliness and order doubtless stemmed from the experience of this summer.

Congenial as the situation at Raymond was, she gave it up at the end of 1870 to become head of a new school, a free public school for Negroes in Clinton. We read in the annual report of the A.M.A. that in its first year (1870) the reconstructed Mississippi legislature had enacted "an excellent free school system." The statement goes on to say that the schools would begin January 1, 1871. However, what seemed "excellent" to the northern A.M.A. did not seem good to the average southern Democrat. Providing free schools for every child was a new idea for Mississippi, an expensive idea too, and to include Negro children, a shocking waste. The man who was to take over as superintendent of education in 1876, after the Reconstruction government was ousted, wrote in 1870 in the *Hinds County Gazette* that the new school law was "an unmitigated outrage upon the rights and liberties of the white people of the State . . . ." In poorer counties where the financial burden of a system of free education seemed unendurable, school houses were burned whether they had been built by the government or by the Negro. (Burning school houses is no new form of protest.) Klansmen were in the saddle, teachers driven away or, if they refused to leave, tortured and sometimes killed.

We can understand why Captain Pease, who had suggested Sarah Dickey's name for the Raymond position, should now as state superintendent of education, turn to her. The system must get off to a good start. He knew Sarah Dickey's excellent training, her drive, and her devotion to the cause of Negro education. Little as she wanted to leave the love and friendship that were hers in Raymond, she yielded to what she felt was God's will for her. She writes, "For some reason the blessed Lord saw fit to remove me from that place [Raymond]. Why he did it, I know not. He knows and I am satisfied."

Clinton, the town to which Sarah Dickey moved in January, 1871, is on a straight line running across the state from Meridian on the east to Vicksburg on the west. It is thirty miles east of Vicksburg and ten miles west of Jackson. At one time it was so much an educational center that it was called the Athens of Mississippi. Before the war there were five schools for "young ladies" and two schools for boys, in addition to Mississippi College, a Baptist institution described as the second oldest (1827) school for men in the state. A major reason for this concentration of schools was Clinton's healthful location on the watershed of the Pearl River to the east and the Black River to the west. Indeed the town was regarded as a health resort in the early days. In 1828 the question of moving the capital from low-lying Jackson, subject to Pearl River floods, to the higher, more healthful Clinton, came up in the legislature. The proposal was defeated by one vote. Two years later the question was settled for good by the building in Jackson of what is now known as the old capitol.

The schools mentioned above had been pretty well disrupted by the war. The only ones left when Sarah Dickey arrived were

Mississippi College and the Central Female Institute. For their survival two New Englanders, Mr. and Mrs. Walter Hillman, were responsible. Walter Hillman had gone South in 1854 after his graduation from Brown University to fill the chair of mathematics and science at Mississippi College, a position to which he had been highly recommended by the president of Brown. He was older than the average college graduate, having had to interrupt his college course from time to time to teach in academies in Massachusetts and Connecticut in order to earn money for his college expenses.

After his first year in Mississippi, he returned to New England only once — to marry. Until his death almost forty years later, he and his wife identified themselves with their adopted state. At the end of his third year at Mississippi College he had resigned to accept the principalship of the Central Female Institute offered him by its trustees. He held many positions of public responsibility — was president of the State Teachers' Association, director of a Jackson bank, became ordained as a Baptist minister just before the war and carried on Baptist services in Clinton during the war. After the war, when the continued existence of Mississippi College looked doubtful, he was made president as the man most able to save it. He did save it. It took him six years, from 1867 to 1873. With his wife's help — she went North to raise funds — he cleared the school of debt, built up attendance from nine students to 190, and in other ways put the college on its feet. Then he resigned to give all his time to his own school.

That school, the Central Female Institute, had been saved during the war by Mrs. Hillman, who, seeking protection for it, had applied directly to General Grant when his headquarters were in Clinton. The guard he placed around it ensured its safety. Later, when Sherman camped nearby, he continued the practice at her request, also protecting the Mississippi College main building, which was then being used as a hospital.

Thus the Hillmans seem to have been able to walk the tight-rope of neutrality. How much sympathy they had at first with Sarah Dickey and her work, we don't know. Dr. Hillman was still president of Mississippi College when she arrived. He apparently was on friendly terms with her in a guarded sort of way if we may judge by a reference she makes in a letter written a year later describing her early experiences in Clinton. She speaks of being "barred out of a store for having walked to meeting on Saturday night with one of the most respectable white citizens of the place." There was no other white citizen in the Clinton of that day who could have so exposed himself to the displeasure of his fellows without censure; but the town was too much indebted to Dr. Hillman to criticize him openly. Individuals, however, could and did show their displeasure to his companion on that walk.

Knowing the Hillmans were Northerners, Sarah Dickey may have applied to them for help when she first came to Clinton and was hunting for a place to live. If she did, they would have told her what she later found out for herself, that no white family was willing to bear the onus of having a lodger who taught in a school for Negroes. Whatever the Hillmans' own feelings may have been, they were unable, because of their school, to help her themselves. However, it is possible that Dr. Hillman spoke of her plight to Senator Charles Caldwell. Whether through the Hillmans or through friends in Jackson, Charles Caldwell learned of Sarah Dickey's need and, as we have said, offered her room and board.

One thing besides his intelligence that set Charles Caldwell off from most of the Negroes of the time was his fearlessness, a rare quality among any people who have been enslaved for generations. This quality may explain why he is even today described in Southern accounts as "arrogant," "notorious," "a daring, desperate negro." But Sarah Dickey, who lived in his house for almost three-and-a-half years, had only good things to say of him. He helped her in many ways, and when she started her own school he was the first president of her Board of Trustees. From the beginning, as we know, she talked over her school problems with him.

There were plenty of problems. She had experiences that would have struck terror to the heart of anyone less dedicated and dauntless. In Vicksburg she had heard much about the ruthless activities of the Ku Klux Klan. Now she received one of the dreaded notices herself. She was ordered to leave Mississippi within ten day or expect to visit her school "through bullets and brickbats and rest under the same treatment at night." She paid no attention to the order. Then one warm night as she was teaching her adult class, she received another warning. She had left the schoolroom door open for air and was standing in the lamplight when suddenly out of the dark came a shot and a bullet flew over her head. She minded this warning no more than she had the first. Next day a prominent citizen explained to her that soon every carpetbagger, man or woman, would have to leave the South. She replied that she had come South to do God's will and could be removed only by death. Her reply was long remembered. At the time of her death more than thirty years later it appeared in a local newspaper article about her. Though she knew her life was in danger, she was not disturbed by the fact. She comments in a letter to a classmate after telling her some of these things, "But how pleasant it is to feel that you are in the right amid all the storms and persecutions."

What she really minded was not physical danger but the social ostracism to which she was subjected. Some women pulled their skirts away from her when they passed her on the street as though to avoid contamination. And occasionally even in church when she would enter a pew, a woman already seated there would leave and take a seat elsewhere. Such things as these cut her to the quick and left her with a devastating feeling of loneliness.

In a letter she wrote to her classmates, dated August 19, 1872, after telling about Raymond she says:

At this place [Clinton] since January, 1871, I have labored under greater difficulties. Oh, the trials, the sore trials, through which I have passed can never be told. Even yet, when I look back over the last twelve months my heart grows sick. Just before the last term closed I made up my mind that I could do nothing better than to shake the dust of Clinton from my feet, but just at the time when it seemed to me I was completely enveloped in Egyptian darkness, the blessed Lord sent a comforting angel. My school closed most triumphantly. Several of the best class of the white people were present at the examination. Two of them addressed the school expressing themselves highly pleased with the exercises.

She includes in this letter a clipping from the *Hinds County Gazette* that had appeared a few days after the close of her school. Under the caption THE COLORED FREE SCHOOL we read the following:

We had the pleasure of attending the examination on Thursday of last week of this school taught by Miss Dickey. . . . We were greatly delighted with the astonishing (to us) progress and thorough educational training of colored children. They stood a good examination that would have done credit to the children boasting Anglo Saxon blood, and so thorough was the discipline and educational system adopted by Miss Dickey that we can safely say her pupils are 'educated not polished' merely, comprehending the idea — the principle of their studies. If Miss Dickey continues to devote herself in this field it may not be many years before her pupils will be critics at the commencement exercises of our high schools and colleges.

The fact that the *Hinds County Gazette* was published in Raymond leads one to surmise that some of the people she met in her year there had followed with interest her work in Clinton.

Such public recognition of her work lifted her spirit and gave her courage to press forward to the realization of her dream. It also smoothed the way for her by calling to the attention of the leading people in Clinton the quality of the work she was doing. Mount Holyoke thoroughness was impressive. In that August 1872 letter she was already able to say, "The prejudices of the white people are being allayed. . . ." At the end she writes, "Next summer I shall begin my lifetime work, that of establishing a Mt. Holyoke Seminary for colored girls. God has appointed me to this great and glorious work, and I shall do it."

5. A Dream Takes Shape

No OFFICIAL document signed and sealed by powerful king or sovereign state could have been more binding than what Sarah Dickey felt was her appointment to found a school for Negro girls in Mississippi. She was convinced that the appointment came from God himself. Over and over she was to say that the school was the Lord's work, not hers. The dream she had at Vicksburg which she had interpreted as meaning that her life work was to be in the great barren field of Negro education had given her the sense of commitment to some special and demanding work. At Mount Holyoke she learned what that work was to be.

She wrote about it in a letter to a classmate in the spring of 1872:

I intend to establish a Mt. Holyoke Seminary for the colored girls. If my debts were paid at Mt. Holyoke I would begin my work next summer. My dear Friend, this is no new thing with me. I have studied about it ever since the first year that I was at the Seminary. I have been here [in Mississippi] these two years for no other purpose than to investigate this matter and to ascertain as to whether it would be expedient to undertake such a measure; and also as to *when* it might be proper to do so. I am fully convinced that the people *need just such an institution,* and that they are ready for it *now.* I also fully anticipate the difficulties which I shall have to encounter, yet when God calls I have no right to plead difficulties as a reason why I should not cheerfully and heartily respond. Hope you will pray that I may be guided aright, that I may be able to begin my work as early as possible and that I may take the right steps at the right time. Hope you will feel interested in my success yourself and that you will interest your friends so much that they will be induced to give me all the aid that they can. . . .

Peace, happiness and prosperity attend our dear classmates in their various callings and avocations. [She sends her love and signs herself]

Fondly, Sarah A. Dickey

Already, though she does not know when or where her school will be, she is arousing interest in it and soliciting aid for it. It would seem from this letter that the *when* was dependent on paying off her indebtedness to Mount Holyoke. That must come first. So, since we know that by the end of the year she felt free to begin her great project, she must somehow have completed her payments. She never speaks of this debt again, though later she fearlessly incurred debts for improvements for the school. It may be that she earned enough in the intervening nine months or that friends came to her assistance. But from whatever source the money came, it is evident that the debt had been canceled. Her sister and her sister's eight-year-old daughter were now living with her at the Caldwells'. She had sent for Mrs. Mather to help her with the "free school" while she was busy raising money and making plans for the school of her dreams.

An amusing by-product of her sister's presence was Sarah Dickey's determination to put an end to the harassment of the Mississippi College students. They thought it fun to ridicule a "nigger teacher," as anyone who taught Negroes was called, and try to crowd her off the sidewalk. Sarah Dickey's method had been to stand stock still and without saying a word let the young men choose, as she put it, between going around or over her. To have her sister annoyed, however, was another matter. As the two of them were returning to the Caldwells' one evening after teaching at night school, a group of students followed them hooting and making insulting remarks. The next day Sarah Dickey set forth armed with a stout cotton umbrella rolled tight. She vowed she would break it over the students' heads if they continued their tactics. The story goes that she met and routed five groups; presumably the determination in her eye, quite as much as the umbrella in her fist, had a subduing effect. Whatever the cause, she and her sister from then on were left unmolested.

But such agitation did not distract her. All the time she was working to realize her dream of a school like Mount Holyoke, but for Negro girls and with a biracial Board of Trustees. Since Negroes had the vote, held office, and were members of the legislature, Sarah Dickey's idea of a biracial Board seemed, if not entirely acceptable, at least in keeping with Republican policy. Yet even so, that she was able to form such a group is remarkable, though less remarkable than that she was able to maintain the racial balance after 1876 when the Democrats took over. She showed Charles Caldwell the list she had prepared of those she might ask to be trustees. It was necessary to have men who carried weight in the community and if possible in the state as well. The three Negroes, spoken of in the preceding chapter, certainly fulfilled these requirements. They were Hiram Rhodes Revels, the man who filled out Jefferson Davis' term in the United States senate, T. W. Stringer, a leader among Mississippi Negroes, and Charles Caldwell. He promised to act as president of the Board of Trustees once it was formed.

Fortunately for us, a list of the first trustees appears on the September 25, 1875, Deed of Trust. In addition to the three Negroes just mentioned and Sarah Dickey herself are three well-known white men. Judge E. W. Cabaniss (also spelled Cabiness), a Clinton resident and faithful friend to the school, served on its Board of Trustees through the entire life of that body. Another Clinton resident was John M. Chilton, a prosperous, friendly planter and store owner. He served as a trustee for at least nine years. The third was A. M. West, a former general in the Confederate army. A prominent businessman, his interests ranged from a scheme to import Swedish peasants to work on Mississippi plantations, a scheme that failed, to managing a railroad, in which he was more successful. He was the trustee instrumental in securing a charter from the state legislature for the projected school. As superintendent of a railroad he supplied Sarah Dickey with passes for her money-raising travels through the state and beyond. Two other railroad superintendents did the same for her, possibly through his influence. About the last three whose names appear on the Deed of Trust, N. G. Gill, H. F. Heighgate, and E. Tucker, we know nothing.

Though they all had told Sarah Dickey they would serve, she ran into difficulty when she tried to get them together to confer about possible sites for the school. Finally she adopted a ruse. Each was asked to meet her at a certain time and place, but nothing was said about others being there too. They all came and evidently were more amused than annoyed by her stratagem. They settled down and found they could work together after all.

Various locations for the school were considered, one of them at Enterprise, a town in the eastern part of the state, a little south of Meridian. But when the project was sounded out in the town itself so much hostility developed that the idea had to be given up. Other possibilities were for one reason or another discarded. Then one of the Clinton members of the Board wondered if the Rices would consider selling their property. They had had a girls' school before the war. Now the small family was rattling around in their spacious thirteen-room house. They might be glad to sell.

The committee to investigate found the place well adapted to their purpose and the owners willing to sell to them. The property consisted of 160 acres on the edge of Clinton, scarcely more than a mile northwest of the railroad station. The main house set high on a knoll in a grove of trees is described from memory by Mr. Courtney Cabell, a former justice of the peace in Clinton, as

a massive colonial structure of red brick. The wide portico was adorned and was conspicuous by enormous white columns. The grounds were beautified by shrubs and flowers in a natural setting of lovely native trees.

Another person spoke of the five handsome marble mantelpieces. One room, perhaps intended for dancing but well adapted to a school assembly room, was twenty-two feet by sixteen. Taken altogether, house and grounds, nothing could have served better the purpose of the proposed school. Mrs. Thomas G. Rice had inherited the place from her father, James Younger, who had bought it from Mrs. Sarah Calvert (spelled also Calvit, Calvitt, and Culbert) for $7,000 in 1856. Mrs. Calvert had bought the land at a tax sale in 1847 and built the large, dignified house on it.

In the abstract of title for the property, it is described first

as "the place known as Peble Hill," but by the time it reaches
the Rices the name Mount Hebron appears in parentheses, and
when the Bargain and Deed of Sale for Miss Dickey's school
are recorded in February, 1874, the item, after the regular section, township and range description, reads "160 acres known
as the Mount Hennon property." This could be a misreading of
Mount Hermon since all documents were in longhand and care-
lessly written *m's, n's,* and *r's* look much alike. Such a possibility
is reinforced by what appeared in the *Jackson Daily News,*
August 20 and 27, 1950, under the caption "Pages from an Old
Scrap Book" by Anabel Power. Speaking of the schools in
Clinton, the author says that Mr. T. G. Rice opened a fashion-
able school for young ladies in Mrs. Calvert's former residence
called Mount Herman Female Institute. That the name already
belonged to the property is further suggested by the fact that
the name of Sarah Dickey's projected school is given in the
April 1873 charter as Mississippi Female Seminary. That also
appears on the February 1874 Bargain and Deed of Sale. But
a year and a half later, on the September 1875 Deed of Trust,
the name is Mt. Hermon Female Seminary. In the interval between the last two dates the name had been officially changed
and recorded. However Sarah Dickey came by the name, it
certainly pleased her by its resemblance to that of her own
dearly loved alma mater. The price settled on was six thousand
dollars, a thousand less than Mrs. Rice's father had paid for it
in 1856. But the aftermath of the war as well as the depression
of 1873 and the fact that Clinton had grown away from this
property and toward Jackson would probably explain the lower
price.

The record in the abstract of title for what is headed *Bargain
and Deed of Sale* reads in part, "Feb. 1874 for $6000 Thomas
and Julia Rice to Charles Caldwell and A. M. West, trustees of
the Mississippi Female Seminary, 160 acres . . . ." The previously mentioned description follows. It is interesting to note that
a colored and a white trustee represented the Board of Trustees
in this important transaction. The property was secured for a
given length of time by the down payment of $10.00, occu-

pancy dependent on the payment of the first $3000. Later two promissory notes are recorded, each for $1500 at 10% interest, the two to cover the second $3000. A former justice of the peace in Clinton told the writer that Mr. Rice didn't really want to sell but felt sure he would recover the property when the full price came due. And in a serial about Sarah Dickey that appeared in three numbers of *Woman's Voice* (vol. VII, 1896) under the title "The Mary Lyon of the South" and for which the author, Elizabeth F. Flagg, interviewed Sarah Dickey, she says that Mr. Rice was disappointed and surprised when full payment was finally made. He had counted on getting the property back plus the three thousand already paid in, feeling sure that a "nigger school" would fail. When this was mentioned to a young woman, a friend of his daughter, she replied that he was not that sort of man at all, that he would have sold the property in good faith. But considering the time of the sale, whatever his motive in selling, he might very naturally have expected his property back. Years later his name appears in a list of people recommending Sarah Dickey and Mount Hermon to possible donors.

A worse time for raising money cannot be imagined. When in 1873 the great banking house of Jay Cooke closed its doors, the resulting panic spread far and wide, and several years of depression followed as business after business collapsed. The revelation of corruption in high places further undermined public confidence. In Mississippi and other Southern states there was a ground swell that soon would topple over the Reconstruction governments. Uncertainty and change were in the air. Money was tight.

Yet Sarah Dickey, in no way dismayed by these adverse conditions, threw herself into the work of raising three thousand dollars with a confidence and enthusiasm that infected her trustees. Mary Lyon had raised the first thousand dollars for *her* seminary by personal solicitation, traveling around among those who would be most benefited by the proposed school. Her first thousand came largely from women. In like manner Sarah Dickey started by traveling around among Negroes in Mississippi, speaking in their churches and soliciting from groups and individuals. In some places she found that the colored people had been warned against her by their white neighbors, who declared her a fraud. But in the main her reception was friendly. She was already known to many through her teaching in Vicksburg and, more recently, in Raymond and Clinton as well as through the recommendations of her colored trustees.

Though most of the Negroes in the state were pitifully poor, they were always willing to sacrifice for their church and for education. Without help they had built out of their meagre earnings their numerous little churches and many of their school houses. The hunger for education among them was a general and genuine hunger. In the American Missionary Association's report for July 1868, figures from the last Freedmen's Bureau report are quoted. Negroes in the South, barely three years out of slavery, had built 364 schools, providing also all the fuel and labor for their upkeep, and in six months had paid in tuition fees $65,319.00. What proportion of this amount came from Mississippi freedmen we do not know, but the figures testify to the freedman's consuming desire for education.

The idea of a seminary for Negro young women, therefore, made an immediate appeal. Collections for it were taken after Sarah Dickey's many talks. Picnics, barbecues, suppers, musicals, and other money-raising entertainments were organized with a will. Friendly white people were also approached. The trustees in the state legislature persuaded their friends among the members to give their pay certificates for one or two days to the cause. There were no large gifts, but in the end the total collected in the state came to a little over a thousand dollars, a surprising sum, all things considered.

Having done what she could in Mississippi, Sarah Dickey headed North. We know she went first to Mount Holyoke because she recorded with pleasure that the first gift she received on the trip was fifty dollars from the president of Mount Holyoke's Board of Trustees, Dr. Edward Kirk. Another gift that pleased her was from her classmates. They had collected money for some sort of class emblem or badge and then decided instead to give half of the money to a classmate working in the foreign field and the other half to Sarah Dickey for her work in the South. She found her share waiting for her on her arrival. Friends in South Hadley gave her letters of introduction to other people and they in turn to still others. She went from town to town, usually staying in the minister's house, collecting a little here and a little there. There must have been something special about her that inspired confidence. Hard-headed New Englanders are not easy to convince. Her biggest gift came not from New England but from her native state. In Cincinnati she was given two hundred dollars worth of furniture for the school. Of this gift she said years later that never did she get so much with so little effort.

This first trip North was a good one even though in the spring of 1875 she had to go again before the whole amount was in hand. By summer she was able to take the first three thousand dollars to the Rices. What a moment that was for her! The three thousand dollars meant that she could take possession immediately and open her school at the regular school-opening time in September. No more delay in beginning her life work. Her heart was full of praise and thanksgiving.

The Rices, on the other hand, were less jubilant. They had not expected the money so soon. The house in Clinton to which they planned to move was not ready. They would like to stay on for a little. Miss Dickey with her sister and niece could move in, of course. There was plenty of room for them all. It was awkward, to say the least, and meant postponing the opening of the school. But Sarah Dickey agreed to the arrangement instead of standing on her rights. She thereby undoubtedly saved the school and possibly even their lives.

The days that followed were busy ones. Sarah Dickey, her sister and niece moved from the Caldwells' on the nineteenth of August. The furniture she had acquired for the school was neatly stacked, waiting the moment of total occupancy, but Sarah Dickey continued, as far as possible, her preparations. She had a hundred things on her mind. She was Board of Admissions, Curriculum Committee, Commissary Department,

Superintendent of Building and Grounds, and much else. The boarding students, already chosen, were waiting for an opening date to be announced.

It was a busy time in town and state, too, for important elections were coming up in preparation for which Republican and Democrat rallies were the order of the day; oratory flourished. A big Republican rally and barbecue was planned for Clinton on September fourth. Charles Caldwell, one of the men in charge, had invited a Democrat, a white man, to make the opening speech, a common act of appeasement at these affairs. Sarah Dickey's niece, eleven years old now, had heard much talk of this great event while they were living at the Caldwells'. She wanted to go and her politically-minded aunt agreed to take her.

September fourth dawned bright and clear, perfect weather for the rally and barbecue on Moss Hill. It had been carefully planned by Senator Caldwell and his associates. No hard drink was to be brought to the grounds and word was passed about among the Negroes that firearms were to be left at home. These restrictions were in the vain hope that incidents leading to brawls might be avoided. There had been in the last year or so an epidemic of so-called "riots," incidents in which racial tension flared into violence. Each riot ended in disaster for the Negro. Here are the mortality figures for some of them: two white men killed, 25 to 30 Negroes; no white man hurt, 12 or 13 Negroes killed; one white man wounded, 6 Negroes killed, etc. As Dr. Vernon Wharton observes in his study of *The Negro in Mississippi, 1865-1890,* "In the political, economic and social subjugation of the freedmen, the most effective weapon ever developed was the 'riot' " (p. 118). That most of the riots were started by white men or boys is no longer in doubt, though the blame was always laid upon the Negro. Each riot left the average Negro more fearful and less likely to offer resistance, for, as Dr. Wharton points out, the years of enslavement had left the freedmen timid and unresourceful as well as economically dependent. Charles Caldwell stood out as a striking exception.

When Sarah Dickey and her niece reached the scene of the Republican rally a great crowd was already assembled from the countryside and neighboring towns. It has been estimated that there were about fifteen hundred Negroes, many of them coming in family groups, more for the barbecue and a day's outing than for the speeches. The white people numbered about a hundred, all of them men and boys with the exception of Sarah Dickey and her niece. The two of them soon found colored friends from Raymond with whom they prepared to listen to the speeches. The first, by the Democrat whom Caldwell had invited, was listened to attentively. Then a white Republican rose. His was to have been one of the main speeches of the day. But he had scarcely finished his preamble when heckling began and trouble quickly followed.

It all developed so quickly that Sarah Dickey was never able to give a clear account. She heard shooting and rebel yells. The men began rushing down the hill to the place where the shooting had begun. She learned later that a colored policeman, seeing two young white men with a whiskey flask, had told them that liquor was not allowed on the grounds and they must leave. The young men, already drunk, replied insultingly. Nearby Negroes entered into the dispute. The young men pulled out their pistols and began shooting. Then finding they were outnumbered, they fled. Unarmed Negroes in hot pursuit caught up with them in a nearby cotton field and killed them. Their bodies found clubbed to death roused the countryside to a fury of rage and fear. Aid was asked from neighboring towns and the Vicksburg "Modocs" were sent for. (This was an organized group of Vicksburg men who took their name from a fierce Indian tribe in northern California that had only recently been subjugated.) Four days of savage revenge followed. The final counting for the day of the riot reads like those already quoted: three white men killed and from ten to thirty Negroes. In the four succeeding days, according to various estimates, from ten to fifty more Negroes were killed.

At the moment, Sarah Dickey was naturally less interested in finding out what had happened than in trying to get her charges out of danger. She had with her not only her niece but two colored friends from Raymond and the child of one of them. Their husbands had joined in the general melee. She managed to get her little group out of reach of the shooting and away from the stampeding, panic-stricken crowds that could so easily have knocked the children down. They reached Mount Hermon, only three quarters of a mile away, without further incident and ate their lunches together, the two children lamenting the abandoned barbecue. Sarah Dickey was sick at heart at the outcome of what was to have been a day of pleasure, but she had no idea as yet of the far-reaching consequences.

When she thought it safe she accompanied her Negro friends to help them find their escorts for the drive back to Raymond. She saw the group started on its way and turned to go back to Mount Hermon. As she drove through the town she was horrified by what she saw. It was full of armed men, the lawless Modocs from Vicksburg and others from neighboring towns. Though they claimed to have been sent for after the trouble began, Sarah Dickey, in telling of it, said she did not see how they arrived as soon as they did unless the trouble had been premeditated and their coming previously arranged.

However that may be, their presence boded ill for the Negroes, who fled in all directions, some to hide in swamps and woods, some to the protection of Governor Ames in Jackson, all leaving their homes and crops to be despoiled. Two were shot just outside the Mount Hermon grounds. Sarah Dickey wondered if they had been on their way to seek sanctuary with her, for Mount Hermon was spared, though only because the Rices were still living there. Worried about her friend Charles Caldwell, Sarah Dickey was relieved to learn that he had managed to reach Jackson and was urging Governor Ames to send for Federal troops. Actually, the governor had already done so and had been told to manage affairs himself with state militia.

So far as Clinton went, with the departure of the Modocs and other armed "helpers," quiet returned to the town. The Negroes began to seep back after those four days of terror and destruction. They repaired as much as possible the damage done to their homes and crops and settled down, albeit uneasily.

The dark days for Sarah Dickey were over, too. She had begun to think that with the Negroes scattered and so much hate and fear in the land, her school might have to be given up even before it began. What had she done amiss that the Lord should have forsaken her? Then her inner voice reproved her, saying "Think, only think!" And she thought what would have happened if she had not left the Caldwells when she did and if she had insisted on opening her school on the first of September as she had so much wanted to do instead of acceding to the Rices's request. She knew then that she had not been forsaken, and the dark moment passed.

The Rices left on the twenty-sixth of September or the day after, for the latter is the date on which she signed the Deed of Trust without which, we are told, the Rices would have been unwilling to leave. She had delayed signing it after they were ready to go until she felt the protection of their presence was no longer needed. So now she was at long last ready to open her school. October fourth was the date set.

But before we come to that great day, there is another matter that must be mentioned because of its consequences. Governor Ames, failing to get federal aid and feeling that he could not trust white soldiers (a consignment of arms that had been sent down the river had been waylaid by them) outfitted a company of colored militia to act as convoy to arms he was sending by wagon to Edwards, a town about twenty-three miles west of Jackson. The company was made up largely of Negroes from Clinton who had fled to his protection at the time of the riot. Charles Caldwell was put in charge. Unfortunately, the road to Edwards passed through Clinton. Made brave by their uniforms and feeling safe under government protection, the colored soldiers marched through the town beating their drums and flying their colors. Nothing could have enraged the citizens more than to see their former slaves in such guise. Added to that feeling was the still unslaked thirst for revenge for the killing of the three white men in the riot scarcely three weeks before. So when the company camped for the night on the outskirts of Clinton, it was with difficulty that the cooler heads in town were able to restrain the many who wanted to attack the company as it slept. The fact that Charles Caldwell headed that company was not forgotten. A day of reckoning was to come. As one writer put it, Caldwell's death warrant was signed on that day.

Overtly, however, all seemed well. A peace agreement between the governor and a committee of responsible citizens was drawn up and signed. According to its terms, the militia was disbanded. Caldwell came home and had his house repaired. It had been sacked by the Modocs who had assured his terrified wife that they would get her husband if it took six years. The experience had left her fearful, though her husband scoffed at the idea of danger and went about as usual. "They may fear me," he said, "but why should I fear them?" It is true that "they" did fear him because of what his testimony might reveal. It was to be given in Washington at an investigation of the so-called "Clinton riot." He would be an important witness.

His main interest now, however, was how he could help Governor Ames, to whom he was devoted, and what, if anything, could be salvaged for the disrupted Republican party from the November elections. They had gone off more quietly than had been feared. The Negro vote was almost negligible, so thorough had been the work of intimidation. The end of the hated Reconstruction government was in sight. A loyal Republican, Sarah Dickey doubtless shared Caldwell's dismay at the turn of affairs. But neither of them realized at first how complete the overthrow of the existing government was to be. A sensible woman, she knew that the mass of Negroes must have more education before they could use power wisely. And her business was education. She and Senator Caldwell put their heads together on ways to make the new school best serve the Negroes' need.

We have no record of the opening day at Mount Hermon Female Seminary. We know the date, October 4, 1875, but that is all we know. How many boarding students were there? We hazard a guess that the ranks were fairly full. For three years it had been talked about in Negro circles, and with three of the five Negro state senators on its Board of Trustees, it must have enjoyed considerable prestige among Negroes. There is much about those opening months that we wish we knew. Since Sarah Dickey had not moved in until August, there could have been little in the way of farm produce for the table later. Did she perhaps can food for the winter while the Rices were there? Or did her Negro friends help supply the table? No answer to any of these questions will probably be found.

Perhaps the last thing that happened in 1875 overshadowed details of earlier, happier days. On the afternoon of December thirtieth Sarah Dickey went to the Caldwells" to consult with the president of her Board of Trustees about certain school matters. The business concluded, she accepted an invitation to stay to supper. Charles Caldwell, she reported later, had been in gay spirits, joking about a difference they had had, but his wife was in a highly nervous state because of a dream on the two previous nights. She was sure that her husband was in some grave danger. He laughingly pooh-poohed her fears, but Sarah Dickey was not so sure. She knew how much his march through town at the head of the colored militia had been resented and how his testimony at the approaching Washington investigation was feared.

So perhaps she was partially prepared when word came to her early the next morning that Senator Caldwell had been killed. She had agreed to meet someone, a teacher one account says, at the railroad station that morning. Telling one of the men to drive to the station and wait for her, she went ahead on horseback to the Caldwells' to see what she could do for the stricken family. As she rode into the town she found the streets again full of the dreaded Modocs, who had been summoned the night before. They started to follow her but then thought better of it, and she went on unmolested. In the parlor at the Caldwells' she found the bullet-riddled body of her friend and also that of his half brother, Samuel Caldwell. And there she learned from the grieving widows and later from others what had happened.

After she had left the night before, Senator Caldwell, without saying what his errand was, had gone down to the village. A white man who, he thought, was his friend had invited him into the basement of Chilton's store, presumably for a holiday drink. An open barred window gave on the street. Thus decoyed, when his "friend" left him, he was shot in the back from the street. The college bell rang, evidently a signal, for crowds gathered and Negroes fled. Too badly wounded to get up by himself, Caldwell called for help, first asking for Judge Cabaniss and then for John Chilton, but neither was there. Finally "Preacher Nelson," a Baptist minister, offered to help him if he would surrender his pistol and promise not to hurt him. When Nelson got him to the street, Caldwell asked to be taken home, but some in the crowd began shooting again and "Preacher Nelson" got out of the way. Caldwell was reported as saying, and Sarah Dickey thought it sounded very like him, "Gentlemen, don't shoot me any more. I am dying anyway, and I want to see my wife." Then when he saw that they were determined to finish him on the spot, his final words were, "All right. Fire away and see how a brave man can die." As "Preacher Nelson" later told Caldwell's widow, "a braver man never lived." Sam Caldwell's death was almost accidental. Unaware of what was happening and in no way implicated in his half brother's affairs, he came riding down the street, was shot off his horse, and beaten to death. The two bodies would have been left in the street but for Dr. Walter Hillman. He knew from the ringing of the college bell that there was trouble abroad and had gone out to investigate. Shocked by what he saw, he had the bodies of the brothers carried to Charles Caldwell's house and then as well as later did all he could for the two women so cruelly widowed.

Sarah Dickey may not have heard the whole story on that first visit. Train time was approaching and she had to leave her bereaved friends. But before she left, Mrs. Sam Caldwell, in the last stages of pregnancy and feeling unable to care for Mary, her headstrong five-year-old daughter, begged Miss Dickey to take the child, "for keeps," she said. Miss Dickey, to comfort her, agreed to take little Mary for the present, at all events. Thus Mary Caldwell became the first in the line of children to whom Sarah Dickey gave a home.

On the road to the station she again met the Modocs, who were returning to Vicksburg by the train from Jackson that Sarah Dickey was meeting. This time she was less fortunate. A "nigger teacher" on horseback seemed fair game to them. So they shot in the air to frighten her horse. The animal reared and tried to get away, but, good horsewoman that she was, Sarah Dickey managed to keep her seat and arrived at the station at a barely controlled gallop. There she asked some of the college boys who were standing around to hold her horse and help her dismount. No one stirred and she had to manage as best she could.

Once her errand at the station was accomplished, the guest or teacher, whichever it was, met and looked out for, she rode slowly back, thinking of what this tragedy meant, not only to the grief-stricken widows, but to the community and to her school. It dangerously widened the breach between colored and white, making more difficult an understanding between them and it left the local Negroes without a leader. As for Mount Hermon, the loss of the president of its Board of Trustees, the man on whom she had most depended, was serious. Where could she find a successor? As she thought over the possibilities, her mind turned to the man who had just showed himself such a friend to the Caldwells. She would ask Rev. Walter Hillman.

It seems probable that two years earlier, when she was selecting her trustees, she would have asked Rev. Walter Hillman to serve. It seems equally probable that he would have refused, for though his six years of pulling Mississippi College out of debt were over, his own neglected school, the Central Female Institute, later known as Hillman College, needed his whole attention. But now the September riot in Clinton, followed by the government overthrow in the November election and finally by this planned murder of Charles Caldwell, whom he respected as an honest and able legislator, would have made him reconsider when Sarah Dickey asked him to take Caldwell's place on the Board. He needed to use his influence for reducing racial tension. Sponsoring a school like Mount Hermon might be one means. He and Sarah Dickey had been thrown much together at this time in their common concern for the Caldwells and had discussed her school and its needs rather thoroughly. In the end he accepted and became president of Mount Hermon's Board of Trustees, a position he held until his last illness.

His greatest value for Mount Hermon lay in his relationship to the town of Clinton. He and his wife, New Englanders though they were, in their more than twenty years in Clinton had become a valued part of the community, looked up to and depended on. He had saved the local college and had proved himself a friend in countless other ways. Any school he sponsored had, by that very fact, some standing in the community. That he was willing to accept the presidency of the Board of Trustees shows his confidence in its founder and her ideas.

But though he had done such fine work in freeing Mississippi College from debt, it must not be assumed that he could help Mount Hermon financially. His earlier work had been as a Baptist minister enlisting the support of northern Baptists for a needy Baptist institution. Also he had his own boarding school to look out for. But what he could and did do for Mount Hermon was of immense importance. Sarah Dickey found that his support made life in Clinton easier in many ways, both for her personally and for the school. The hazardous first steps had been taken and now Mount Hermon Seminary was an accepted institution in the community. The long cherished dream was no longer a dream, it was a reality.

6. Life at Mount Hermon

ALTHOUGH MOUNT HERMON SEMINARY in its beautiful setting was now accepted in the community and no longer in danger of being destroyed by mob violence, its founder and principal could not sit back and enjoy the realization of her dream. That dream, so improbable and unsubstantial when it had first come to her ten years earlier in her student days at Mount Holyoke, was now a reality and a very demanding reality. Problems met her at every turn — and emergencies.

The first five years were hard ones. Twenty years later she describes them in this way. (She has been telling of the Clinton riot of 1875 that delayed the opening of the school.)

> During the next five years, with never more than one or two helpers, I did a great deal of the teaching, about all of the preaching, managed everything, working a great deal with my own hands — in doors and out, and raised the other $3,000 on the purchase price of the property, and about $1,000 more for repairs, furnishing, etc., friends, — Job's friends — on every hand awaiting the failure. But failure never came. God will never fail to take care of His own.

She does not even mention here the scourge of yellow fever that struck the South when Mount Hermon was scarcely three years old. The epidemic of 1878 was unusually severe. Negroes, as always, were hardest hit, and those at Mount Hermon were not spared. Just what happened at the Seminary we do not know. Was the school closed or did it manage somehow to carry on? We can get some idea of how devastating the experience was by reading between the lines of a letter Sarah Dickey wrote nearly ten years later to her church paper, the *Religious Telescope*. She was begging for help, but first she began by telling how much the United Brethren had already done for Mount Hermon. She says,

In 1879, after the yellow-fever season of 1878 had left us in destitute circumstances, you went all over the country — north, east, and west — searching for help for us, and you worked faithfully until you had helped us clear out of our distresses.

Another sort of emergency had a more lasting effect on Mount Hermon. It came from the closing of the Clinton "free school for blacks" where Sarah Dickey had taught and the consequent plea of a group of Negro parents that Miss Dickey let their children attend her school. The free school had continued for the first year or so after the southern Democratic government came into power in 1876. A series of riots like the Clinton riot had so intimidated the Negro that his vote was negligible, and consequently the hated Republican Reconstruction government was "out."

Interestingly enough, retained from the discredited and despised Reconstruction government was what had been most violently opposed when in 1870 the public school law was passed. The man who had called the law "an unmitigated outrage" was now, as superintendent of education for Mississippi, administering it. He still thought it folly to educate Negroes at public expense, but according to the constitution it was the price that must be paid if white children were to benefit. There was no need, he thought, to pay too much attention to the Negro schools. Thus was initiated the erosion of neglect that continued until relatively recent times. The number of schools and the teachers' salaries were reduced. The salary reductions were progressive. Dr. Wharton in the book already cited says that from an average of $55.00 a month in the Reconstruction years Negro teachers received $40.00 in 1876 and on down to $21.53 in 1895.

Just why the school in Clinton was given up is not known. It may have been closed at the time of the smallpox epidemic and never opened again or it may be that Superintendent Gathright thought one school for Negroes in a town was enough, regardless of the fact that the school he referred to was a private residential seminary for young women.

But when the Negro parents begged Sarah Dickey to take in their boys and girls as day students, there was no question in her mind as to what she must do. Any need she could supply had a claim on her. Actually, taking in the village children was not so difficult as might be supposed, for many of her students of whatever age had to begin at the ABC level. Their ex-slave parents were illiterate, of course. Except for some mission schools and the brief life of the Freedmen's Bureau there had been no chance for education until 1871 and the Reconstruction schools. During the four stormy years that followed, the Ku Klux Klan made Negro schools their special target. They drove out teachers as they had tried to drive out Sarah Dickey, and they set fire to Negro school buildings and to churches also if schools were held in them. (A familiar pattern this — thirty-eight Negro churches were burned in Mississippi during 1964.) In some counties not a Negro schoolhouse was left standing. Under such circumstances Mount Hermon could expect very little if anything in the way of preparation from her early students.

The elementary work was already organized and in operation when Sarah Dickey granted the parents' request and opened Mount Hermon to the village boys and girls. In one of the annual catalogues she explains that although Mount Hermon

was intended, of course, for girls only, at the earnest solicitation of the parents, the boys of the neighborhood have been admitted as day pupils. And as we can teach them here without detracting in the least from the highest interests of the girls' boarding-school department, we feel that it is only right and just to allow them the privilege of the best advantages for education that they can have in the vicinity.

Not just the best advantages, but for a long time Mount Hermon provided their only opportunity for education.

There may have been some financial arrangement with the town, but no records were kept. Twenty years later the Seminary received fifty cents a pupil, a sum later still increased to a dollar. It is not clear whether this lordly amount was for a term or a year. Perhaps at first the Negroes themselves paid a

small fee for their children's tuition, as they had done in Vicksburg. Such an arrangement would have been in keeping with
Sarah Dickey's ideas and practices. She worked to develop independence and self-respect among a people who had had little
experience of either.

Though these day students were not part of the dream Sarah
Dickey had cherished, not those for whom the school had been
established, she threw herself into work for them that went far
beyond teaching the three R's. That part she left largely to her
pupil teachers. But when it came to building good habits, to
instilling ideas of honesty, to laying foundations for good
citizenship, she never missed an opportunity. She was always
thinking of ways and means to help the day students as well as
her seminary "young ladies." For instance, in a letter to her
church paper, the already mentioned *Religious Telescope,* she
says,

We are greatly in need of a bell — a great big bell. Our people have
no clocks, and our children from the neighborhood are either an hour
more or less, too early, both to day-school and Sunday School, or too
late — usually too early; for woe be unto them if they are too late,
especially to the day-school; and it is unprofitable to them and to their
parents, and uncomfortable to us, to have them here so much too early.
We want a bell that we may more effectually teach them promptness.
We have realized in our Sunday School, in nickels and dimes, some
twenty-five or thirty dollars for a bell; but we want one that will cost
four or five times as much, and we hope somebody will help us get it.

Somebody did, a Miss Kate Emerick of Middletown, Ohio, who
became a good friend of Mount Hermon Seminary. The large,
handsome brass bell was mounted on the seminary grounds. It
not only called the children to school in the morning, but in the
afternoon it sounded forth to let the mothers know when school
was out. Alas for those who loitered too long by the way! The
mothers and Sarah Dickey were in close alliance. Before the
installation of the bell she sometimes had driven to town behind
the children to make sure they went home directly and in an
orderly way.

These village children were incorporated into the life of the
Seminary in various ways. They attended the daily chapel serv-

ice and had part in the final exercises of the school. Their names appear in the annual catalogue. Because of the Southern custom of frequently giving girls surnames as first names and sometimes even boys' names, it is impossible to tell from these catalogue lists how many boys received their education at Mount Hermon Female Seminary. The fact that Sarah Dickey later built a dormitory for the small boys shows that Mount Hermon's hospitality was not limited to the village boys.

For some of these children Mount Hermon was more than a school. It was their home. As we have seen, Sarah Dickey's response to any need she was able to fill was immediate and practical. Witness the way she took in five-year-old Mary Caldwell in Mount Hermon's very first year. Mrs. Sam Caldwell was not the only Negro mother who was glad to give her child to Sarah Dickey to bring up. Since it was against the law for a white man to leave anything to his colored mistress and his children by her, both mother and children might be left destitute. Willette Campbell, for instance, had led a happy, protected childhood until her father, a wealthy and kindly white man, suddenly died. Mount Hermon was the answer. A gifted student, Willette graduated from the Normal Course, taught there and was married at the Seminary. Alma and Charlie Chapman, children of a white father, were given home and education by Sarah Dickey. Eddie Messenger was another, a promising lad whom she later sent to Tougaloo for further education. Then, too, there were those recommended by white people, teachers from the North and others. They knew Sarah Dickey's generous nature and the good training the children would get at Mount Hermon. Today in Mississippi at the Piney Woods Country Life School, Dr. Laurence Jones does much the same thing on a larger scale for needy Negro children.

Among those Sarah Dickey brought up, two deserve special mention. Together they cover the entire life of the Seminary up to the time of her death. Their memories have greatly enriched this biography. The first is Mary Caldwell, already mentioned, whose mother, about to bear her third child at the time her husband was murdered, felt herself unequal to handling her

eldest. Little Mary at the age of five had already shown herself
to be independent and hard to manage. However, the child
adjusted well to the busy life at Mount Hermon. Miss Dickey
put her in a room next to her own. They shared closet space
and washing arrangements. She sat by her foster mother at
table and was served first. She followed Miss Dickey about and
was taught to help where she could, the bursting energy that
so overwhelmed her mother being directed to useful ends. She
had a large part in the life of Mount Hermon during its first
seventeen years.

The writer knew her as Mrs. Mary Caldwell Coats, a widow
for thirty-five years. A vigorous, brusque, rather taciturn woman
in her eighties, keeping a very tidy rooming house in Jackson,
she was just beginning to talk more freely about her life at
Mount Hermon when an accident caused her sudden death. Had
she lived longer this account of the early days at the Seminary
would be more complete. Fortunately she had already drawn
some vivid pictures of that time.

One picture takes us back to the first or second year of Mount
Hermon before there were boys in the school to chop and carry
wood for the many fireplaces and stoves with which the rooms
were heated. The damp cold of a Mississippi winter made fires
necessary. Mrs. Coats told about going out in the cold with
Miss Dickey while the latter chopped kindling. Mary was too
small to lift the heavy axe, but she could drag it along and she
could pick up the kindling and carry some of it into the house.
As she grew older she was taught to milk the cows and curry
the horses and, of course, she had many duties about the house.
Evidently she was a practical, responsible child on whom Sarah
Dickey could depend. By the time she was fifteen, she was a
sort of acting matron in the school, but she had by no means
outgrown the need for correction. On one occasion she and
Miss Dickey had a regular tussle — "tussle" was her word.
Miss Dickey had picked up a buggy whip with which to punish
her — she didn't remember what she had done. She seized hold
of the whip and wouldn't let go until Miss Dickey promised not
to use it on her. "You could always trust Miss Dickey's word,"

she said. "She played fair." So she let go and was punished in some other way. When she told how Miss Dickey had once admitted to being in the wrong and apologized to her, there was still surprise and admiration in her voice. She had been corrected before some of the girls over whom she was in charge. She objected, not to the correction but to the publicity of it. After thinking over her objection, Miss Dickey agreed with her and begged her pardon.

This matter of punishment was interesting to explore. Those questioned gave very different replies. One said that Miss Dickey could shame you by the way she talked to you. "She took time to tell you good." Several spoke of being locked in their rooms and missing dinner. One remembered washing windows as a penalty. One, who had lived in the Seminary for two years, could not remember that Miss Dickey ever whipped anyone. But there is plenty of evidence that she did whip as well as spank. The little girls were put across her knee and spanked with a ruler. Whipping was reserved for "really bad things like telling lies and stealing." It was usually done with "doubled over switches from trees." A day student recounted the following experience. It seems that an old vagrant called Aunt Cheney, whom Miss Dickey had taken in, was very ill one day and Miss Dickey had dismissed school in order to take care of her. Agnes, the narrator, and Minnie, her friend, enjoyed the holiday so much that they decided to prolong it by taking the next day off too. When Agnes' mother asked her why they were home so early on that second day, she made the reply they had agreed on, that Aunt Cheney had died. Her mother spotted the lie immediately. If Aunt Cheney had died the seminary bell would have been tolled, she pointed out, and promised her daughter a good whipping. But her father, who tended to spoil his only daughter, counseled delay to make sure. So the next day her mother took her to school and found out the truth. Miss Dickey, however, said she would do the whipping. First she took the two girls into her office and talked to them. Then she had them bare themselves to the waist. She took her horsewhip and laid on so hard that Agnes' mother had to grease the welts. Next she prayed with them and then the three of them sang a hymn. Minnie was made sullen by the punishment, but Agnes had always been grateful for it. She said, "Started me on the right road, she did. She was a real Christian," and she looked lovingly at the framed photograph of Sarah Dickey hanging above the fireplace that heated her cabin. "Yes, she sure was a real Christian."

Examining these so various accounts of Sarah Dickey's methods of punishment, one sees that two factors always entered in — the nature of the misdemeanor and the nature of the culprit. Lying was far more serious than an infraction of house rules though the latter might affect more people and cause greater inconvenience. Also Sarah Dickey seems to have relied less on corporal punishment as she grew older and more on moral suasion. From the reminiscences of Mrs. Coats it would appear that Miss Dickey had a quick temper, but later students spoke of her as being even tempered. Undoubtedly little Mary was a difficult child, stubborn, full of energy, and self-willed. She must often have tried Sarah Dickey's temper. Perhaps the experience with her helped Sarah Dickey to acquire that control of her feelings which was later remarked on.

Certainly they both learned to get along together and were mutually helpful. Mrs. Coats took pride in telling how when visitors came she was the one to be called out of class to show them around. She graduated from the Normal Course in 1891 and was married soon after at Mount Hermon, where Miss Dickey gave her "a real nice wedding" and where she continued to live for two or three more years. Her first baby was born there, buried there too. Then she and her husband moved to Jackson. When Miss Dickey had business in the city, she would drive to Mary's house and Mary would unhitch and feed the horses while Miss Dickey rested before going about her errands. When she came back, her business completed, Mary gave her a good meal, harnessed the horses and watched her drive off.

One story Mrs. Coats would not have told had she not been asked about it particularly. Various people, none of whom was around when it happened, had recounted it. To check it with a firsthand account seemed desirable. For once the reports agreed with the facts. It seems that one of Mary's duties was to go to town daily for the mail. The sidewalks in Clinton at that time were made of two wooden planks laid lengthwise. The streets were unpaved and often muddy. They were muddy on the day Mary Caldwell and a friend who was with her saw a fine lady approaching them. They didn't know who she was. Instead of stepping into the mud and waiting till she passed, they fell into single file on one of the planks, leaving the other for the lady. That meant that their skirts brushed hers as they passed. Furious, the lady turned back to the post office — she was the postmaster's wife —and told her husband what had happened. He came out immediately and, seizing a whip from the stand of a neighboring harness shop, he gave the two girls a thorough beating right there on the main street of Clinton in the middle of the morning when shoppers were about. He even knocked Mary Caldwell down with the handle of the whip.

The publicity of the humiliating and painful experience still rankled sixty-five years later and made Mrs. Coats reluctant to talk of it in spite of the triumphant ending. For Sarah Dickey, when the girls returned and told her what had happened, went into immediate action. She consulted one of her lawyer friends with whom she did business. In a little more than a month the postmaster was out of a job. That is why the Negroes so much rejoiced in the story and kept it alive. For us its significance lies in its evidence of the place Sarah Dickey had won in the white community that had once so scorned her. We can date the affair, for Mary Caldwell was fifteen at the time, which would make it about 1885. Incidentally, Mary Caldwell was sent for the mail alone after this experience, and on horseback.

The second person, the one whose life at Mount Hermon covered the second half of the Seminary under Sarah Dickey, is Mr. Claude Inge of Jackson, Mississippi, a retired builder. He and his wife, a Normal Course graduate, have contributed more than anyone else to this study. They knew, admired and loved Miss Dickey and Mount Hermon. Mr. Inge died in the fall of 1963 at the age of eighty-two.

Sometime toward the end of 1889 Sarah Dickey received a letter from a friend, an A.M.A. teacher in Mobile, Alabama, telling her about the sad plight of a Negro family by the name of Inge. The father and mother had both died of tuberculosis leaving two girls of an age to profit by a Mount Hermon education and a little eight-year-old boy. A young married sister could not care for them and there was very little money for their education. Could Miss Dickey find room for them? Sarah Dickey's immediate response was characteristic. She took a train to Mobile and brought the three of them back with her on January 27, 1890. Mr. Inge treasured a small worn notebook in which Sarah Dickey had carefully entered the date and the expenses of the trip. Tickets for the three came to $9.45. Her own round trip ticket cost $9.30. One of the girls, Maud, had already contracted her parents' disease and died that very spring. The notebook tells us that Sarah Dickey paid half ($10.00), on "Maudie's" coffin; the other half came from the married sister. The younger girl, Virginia, lived only long enough to graduate from the Normal Course and help out briefly as student teacher before she too died of the same disease. The girls were buried on the grounds in a plot Miss Dickey had chosen as a graveyard. In the official Hinds County record of cemeteries it is listed as Dickey Cemetery. Maud's grave was the first one there.

With Virginia's death the only one left of the family Sarah Dickey had so hopefully transplanted was Claude, a delicate child to whom she gave the love and care she would have given a child of her own. He well repaid her. To him she was indeed like a real mother. Mount Hermon was his home; its concerns were his concerns. It provided him with much more than an education. As he grew up he was first a handy boy about the place and then a handyman performing all sorts of useful services. He took care of the horses: Dolly and Daisy, a sorrel span; Sherman and Grant, an earlier pair ready to be retired; and Billy and Beauty, the two raised on the place. He was allowed to ride Billy whenever he wanted to. And he was the one who drove Miss Dickey on many of her errands. She had him learn the carpenter's trade because it would provide a good livelihood for him and doubtless be of help to her at Mount Hermon.

Claude Inge lived at the Seminary until he was twenty-two. Then he left for a job in Arkansas. That was late in December of 1903. Sarah Dickey was ill at the time and he expected to find her in bed. When he went to her room to bid her good-bye, she wasn't there. He finally located her on the third floor directing two men who were making repairs. She kissed him goodbye, gave him words of encouragement, and he left, never to see her again. She died less than a month later. "The finest woman I've ever known," was his comment when he spoke of his loss. According to his widow, some sixty years later his own deathbed was brightened by happy dreams of his dear Miss Dickey.

Not all the children Sarah Dickey took turned out so well as these two. She had her quota of failures. There was Arthur, an orphan, whom she expected to bring up; he ran away when she whipped him, never to return. There was little Spencer, sent to her from Mobile by the teacher who had written her about the Inges. Though only seven, he had already acquired some vicious habits and a considerable fund of profanity. Try as hard as she could, she seemed unable to do anything with him. He was even corrupting some of the other children. A man who was a boy at that time shook his head at mention of the child. "Spencer was a really bad boy, through and through." She finally had to return him to his Mobile sponsor.

Nor was all smooth sailing with her seminary "young ladies." Perhaps she felt worst about Beatrice, the fifteen-year-old girl whose brother had brought her to Mount Hermon, paying her fees for the year. Some of the students thought she was preg-nant and told Miss Dickey so. But Sarah Dickey discounted their suspicion. So did the girl's roommate who was up with her several nights when she was restless, suffering from "tooth-ache," she said. But on the night the baby was born, the roommate slept right through. The girl somehow managed things herself, killed the baby and, wrapping it in a cloth, put it high on a ledge above a doorway in the hall before she made off. There Claude Inge found it the next morning. Sarah Dickey drove immediately to the railroad station. But the girl had evidently caught an earlier train. Her brother was sent for and a search made, but as far as those at Mount Hermon knew, no trace of her was ever found.

These failures, however — and there must have been others — are scarcely to be mentioned in view of the impact that her training and personality made on most of her students and through them on the community at large. It is fascinating to watch the process — the conditions she found and how she changed them. A leaflet written in the early days of the Seminary describes what she found. Referring to the freedmen it says,

Their home life is the one room cabin; their household duties, the corn cake and boiling-pot; their laundry, the field kettle and picketfence; their wardrobe, the tattered garment or purchased ready-made apparel. They need a *thorough drill* in *every department* of *industry* and *household economy.*

Organizing dormitory life among young women accustomed to such conditions presented a problem. But here Sarah Dickey's Mount Holyoke years stood her in good stead although changes and adaptations were necessary for students coming from such a different background, whose experience of group living, even as members of a family, was limited. She could take nothing for granted. Personal habits, standards of conduct, speech, dress, preparation and serving of meals, care of house and rooms, social life — all must be planned and supervised. She organized the daily life so carefully that the plan needed little change as time went on.

The rising bell that Mary Caldwell rang at five o'clock in the early days was later rung by others at six; the seven o'clock breakfast was changed to seven-thirty. All gathered for chapel at eight-thirty, and then from nine to twelve attended classes. After a hearty noonday dinner classes were held again till three-thirty. At that time the students turned their attention to the care of the buildings. Earlier in the day, between rising and breakfast, they had taken care of their own rooms and certain of them had set the tables and prepared breakfast. After breakfast and before chapel some groups had washed the breakfast dishes; others had taken care of the teachers' rooms. Still other groups were responsible for dinner and supper. This afternoon work was different. It had to do with keeping floors, woodwork and windows spotless. It involved much scrubbing and polishing and was carefully supervised. Each student had her own afternoon each week for washing her clothes. After the laundry was built the place must have been full of afternoon chatter and gaiety with as many as twenty girls washing their clothes at the same time, ten on each side. An early supper and a nine o'clock bedtime completed the day.

The "family arrangements," as Miss Dickey called them, were closely modeled on Mount Holyoke's so-called domestic work system. But while Mary Lyon stressed the fact that her plan of cooperative housework was simply for the purpose of reducing the expense of education and in no sense intended to take the place of, or even supplement a girl's training in her own home, Sarah Dickey regarded the necessary work as an integral part of her students' education. "It is a well-known fact," she says in one of the Mount Hermon catalogues, "that the industrial education of young people of the South is equally important as their literary training." We read in some of the seminary catalogues of a special teacher of sewing and another listed as teacher of cooking and housework.

The meals produced under this system were described as "very good" by Mrs. Mary Caldwell Coats and also by various later residents. Breakfast consisted of grits, of course, bacon and eggs, and, instead of Southern hot bread (biscuit, muffins, or rolls), Northern "cold light bread," as ordinary white bread was called. No coffee — Miss Dickey didn't drink it — but there was always plenty of milk. For dinner there might be beef (this had to be bought, a half or a whole animal at a time), pork (Mount Hermon raised its own hogs), chicken or turkey (home grown), sweet potatoes, turnips, cabbage, tomatoes, and plenty of home canned fruit. Plums and blackberries grew on the grounds; other fruit was donated or bought. During the canning season from a hundred to a hundred and fifty cans would be put up a day. Miss Dickey was a master hand at canning fruit we are told; others did the vegetables and pickles and salted down the cabbages. Supper was a light meal, but no one seemed to remember what was served.

The work was carefully organized and supervised, each girl holding her assignment from four to six weeks and then passing on to another task. The one exception was the bell ringer, a popular office. If she was a minute late, she was immediately replaced. Punctuality was insisted on, a new concept to most of the students. One of the boys Sarah Dickey had brought up said, and he was a man in his seventies at the time, that he had never been late to anything in his life, so thoroughly had Miss Dickey impressed on him the virtue of promptness.

To her success along other lines, too, the writer can personally testify. All the houses and cabins that she visited, unannounced, to talk to former Mount Hermon students were, with one exception, neat and spotlessly clean. Though the one exception was clean enough, it had the sort of disorder she was familiar with in her own home. In their talks all stressed how well Mount Hermon was kept — "tiptop condition," "shining clean," "spotless" were some of the terms used. Another point they made was how well organized the work was. "It ran easy-like." The picturesque Mount Holyoke terminology (Blue Crockery Circle, etc.) was not used, but the plan was like Mount Holyoke's though the groups were of necessity smaller. For instance, after meals one group washed the china, one the glassware, one the "silver," and one the pots and pans. A 1901 Normal Course graduate who had been a successful teacher in the years between remembered just what she did when it was her turn to take care of a teacher's or a visitor's room. (She said a good many visitors came from the North and spent a day or so at the school.) After breakfast she would clean the room, empty the "slops," fill the water pitcher, and make the bed. In the afternoon she opened the window; after supper she closed the shutters and turned down the bed. In her day it was Miss

Taylor, of whom more later, who saw that all was properly done.

On Sundays after a later breakfast and the usual household chores there was Sunday school, attended also by townfolk. Then the students were free to go to the church of their choice, returning for a hearty noonday dinner and an hour of quiet before the afternoon preaching service in the Mount Hermon chapel. A visiting colored preacher from Jackson or some other town conducted the service which was open to the public, thus giving the countryside a greatly appreciated opportunity to hear different ministers. The final service of the day came after the Sunday night supper and was especially for the boarding students. Miss Dickey presided and always spoke. These talks, as well as what she said in the morning chapel, made a deep impression. As her former students talked about them more than fifty years later, some seemed almost to be quoting her very words. Also remembered were the many Bible passages, sometimes whole chapters, that they had learned and recited so often that for some of the women I talked with they had become permanent possessions. Sarah Dickey found many opportunities for fixing the passages in memory. Occasionally while standing by their places at breakfast or supper, each student would recite a verse of her own choosing. More often the first would begin with the first verse of a chapter they all knew, the next the second, and so on to the end of the chapter. The daily chapel exercises might include at times Bible quotations. The passages most often mentioned were the three chapters in Matthew dealing with the Sermon on the Mount, the fourteenth chapter of John ("Let not your heart be troubled"), the thirteenth of First Corinthians ("Though I speak with the tongues of men and of angels"), various Psalms and the last chapter of Proverbs from the tenth verse to the end. From this chapter about the virtuous woman Sarah Dickey chose the text used on the Mount Hermon diploma and certificates, a use in the Mount Holyoke tradition.

In the students' week there was still another religious service, the Tuesday evening vespers. It consisted of Bible reading or recitation, singing, prayer, and a talk by one of the teachers. A former student described the time when two or three of them tried to skip this service. They were missed and a teacher sent to look for them. "My, we sure got to chapel fast that time!" They were more successful with the time-honored school-girl practice of covering their transom, staying up beyond the nine o'clock bedtime, and making candy on the stove that heated their room.

Friday evenings were popular, given over to a "literary" program — recitations, reading, original essays, piano and organ pieces and singing. These evenings were used in part as preparation for the exercises on the great days at the end of the school year. A favorite feature recalled by a former student who remembered both the words and the gestures was the reading of a dramatic poem by a student or teacher accompanied by a small group who illustrated in pantomime what was read. Vocal music became a part of all three courses of study every year, and the song book was added to the Bible and dictionary as required possessions.

There were informal occasions, too, for song. When there was sickness in the neighborhood, Miss Dickey would take a few of the girls to sing to the patient. After the singing, she would kneel by the bedside and pray and then leave the soup or home canned fruit she had brought. If the illness was within the walls of the Seminary, she was quite likely to act as doctor, too. Those were the days when homeopathy flourished. She kept a supply of homeopathic medicines — aconite, pulsatilla, belladonna, nux vomica— which she seems to have administered wisely.

Though the day-students could not have part in some of these activities, especially the evening ones — some of them lived as much as four or five miles away and one trudged eight miles to school — they came out in full force on Sunday and also had active share in the daily chapel service. One day-student described how when the village children heard the first bell ring in the morning, they would start running. By the time the last bell sounded, they were all there, forming in line to march into chapel singing.

All these many exercises and activities culminated during the third week of May in three momentous days, momentous not just for students and teachers, marking the end of a successful school year, but for the Negroes in the surrounding countryside as well. For many of them it was the big event of the year. Families came by the wagonload from every direction. A man who grew up in Vicksburg remembered that as a boy he had looked forward to the Mount Hermon commencements. Several wagonloads went from Vicksburg, he said. They took two days for the thirty-mile journey, stopping for the night at Edwards. There was much to enjoy in the three days that followed. The public oral examinations of the first two days followed the custom of the final Mount Holyoke examinations. They must have been a source of racial pride to the audience, for the students had been thoroughly drilled and were at their best. On the first day the exercises of the primary school, or preparatory, as it was later called, were held. Here is where the day students had an opportunity to show what they had learned. On the evening of the second day came the concert, an especially fine affair, all home talent and by no means limited to musical numbers. Essays and recitations with and without the pantomime described were also included. The music was both vocal and instrumental. When the group graduating from the Normal Course was large enough, there were the usual class prophecy, poem, and history. The audience took special pleasure in this so-called concert. Then on the morning of the last day came the graduation exercises, sometimes with an outside speaker, and the presentation of certificates to those who had finished the Normal Course.

When it was all over, there were sandwiches and lemonade on tables set up on the lawn. In 1901, according to one informant who graduated that year, eight tables outdoors, each spread with tablecloth and set for eight people, accommodated the families and friends of the graduates. Others brought their own lunches to eat under the trees. These refreshments marked the end of the happy days. Mules were backed into wagons, horses into buggies and surreys. Families piled aboard and drove away in a haze of pleasant memories.

A passage from a letter written nearly ten years after Sarah Dickey's death by one of the two teachers left in the greatly diminished school shows how the Negroes counted on these days. The writer, explaining how overworked she is, complains that "The community expect grand closing exercises as usual."

What these days of "grand closing exercises" meant to the Negro community is hard to put into words. It is not just that they made a break in the dull routine of daily lives, important as that service was. They did much more. The fact that their young people were having opportunities that the older Negroes had never had and were showing what they could do made them all proud. And perhaps most important of all was the effect of Mount Hermon on them. It was theirs in a special sense, a beautiful place where they could be their best selves, the equal of anybody.

7. Problems

DEEPLY SATISFYING as Mount Hermon was to those for whom it had been established, it fell lamentably short in two crucial matters of being the school "like Mount Holyoke" that Sarah Dickey felt herself commissioned to build. In the almost thirty years of her administration she was never able to develop a student body for what she regarded as the seminary proper, a three year course, later reduced to two years, based on the Mount Holyoke curriculum and leading to a diploma of graduation from Mount Hermon Female Seminary. Only one such diploma was ever granted. Nor, though Sarah Dickey accomplished miracles in meeting running expenses, keeping buildings in repair and erecting new ones, was she ever able to ensure permanence for Mount Hermon by either raising an endowment for it or finding an organization to take it over.

In view of the conditions Sarah Dickey met on her return to Mississippi, she planned the studies for her school in three steps or courses leading to the Mount Hermon diploma. The initial step was the necessary elementary work of the first four grades. Next came a three-year course beginning with the Fifth Reader and leading to the third step, a final three-year course called at first Higher English Course, a name later changed to Advanced Course. This was the course expected to develop into a Mississippi Mount Holyoke.

The 1882-'83 catalogue says of this course:

The studies in this course are of high grade, and when properly mastered will give the student a truly liberal education. This course occupies three years, and those who complete it will be entitled to a Diploma from the Seminary.

At the end of the same catalogue pupils are urged to take the full course and graduate since "it will be impossible to do themselves justice with anything short of the Higher English Course."

But when after ten years no student had managed to do herself that kind of justice or even so much as to begin the course, Sarah Dickey, practical as well as patient, saw she must make some adjustments. She shortened the course by a year and added Latin, apparently in response to a local request. It was then the name was changed to Advanced Course. The Mount Holyoke pattern, cut down to scale, was still kept — the yearly requirement of Bible and English composition (vocal music was added to this group), the emphasis on science, and courses such as moral philosophy and evidences of Christianity.

These changes seem to have helped, for in 1887 a student named Julia Brown enrolled in the Advanced Course, continued through the two years and in 1889 received the one and only diploma Mount Hermon ever granted. From all accounts Julia Brown was an unusually gifted person. The next year she returned to teach at Mount Hermon and made a very special place for herself. It was of her that Sarah Dickey wrote, "The best teacher we have turned out was also the best worker in all kinds of housework." She had plans for sending Julia away for further training that she might some day perhaps be able to take over the Seminary. Julia Brown's early death, like the deaths of several other of her promising students, defeated her happy plans for them and must have filled her with a sense of personal loss.

In the wake of Julia Brown an occasional student enrolled in the Advanced Course, but never for more than the first year. However, Sarah Dickey did not give up hope nor did she lower her standards. It might take much longer than she had expected to accomplish what the voice had told her to do. A full description of the Advanced Course continued to appear in the annual catalogues as long as she lived. It was a goal set before the students. Julia Brown had reached it; in God's good time others would follow; Mount Hermon some day would become the

Mississippi Mount Holyoke of her dream. Her patience was inexhaustible and her faith never wavered.

While waiting for that happy day she put her energies on the second course, the course that began with the Fifth Reader. In the 1882-'83 catalogue, before any changes were made, the following astonishing statement appears:

Those who finish this course will have a good understanding of the branches taught in the common schools of the state, and be prepared to occupy positions as teachers in such schools.

What revealing comment this is on the common schools of Mississippi at that time! The statement becomes somewhat less astonishing when we realize that the young ladies of the Seminary were older than our sixth or seventh graders, that the seminary school year was seven months as compared to the common schools' three or four, and also when we recall the thorough teaching methods Sarah Dickey had imported from her alma mater. What her young ladies knew they knew well. From a report written in 1881 by a Northern visitor, Rev. W. J. Shuey (of whom more later) we learn that of the four hundred students who had attended Mount Hermon in the first six years, no less than fifty were teaching in the public schools of the state. Yet not one of those fifty had completed even the modest work outlined for the three years of the Preparatory Course, as the second course was at first called. Such facts and figures make it clear that there was no incentive for prospective teachers to go on to the "liberal education" planned for them. Sarah Dickey, therefore, set about strengthening the second course. She changed its name from Preparatory Course to Normal Course, thereby admitting that it was an end in itself, and she enriched its offerings. Among the subjects added were hygiene, physiology, algebra, botany and theory and practice of teaching. Bible and English composition appear in each of the three years, the Mount Holyoke influence again asserting itself. Instruction in piano became available at three dollars a month extra; organ, at two dollars a month. A catalogue statement reads, "Piano and organ students will receive two lessons a week, and will be required to practice from one to two and a half hours a day."

In the 1892-'93 catalogue six organ students and eleven piano students are listed. This same catalogue promises that

Each pupil who completes the Normal or Teachers' Course satisfactorily will receive from the Seminary a Certificate of graduation from that Course. The studies in this Course are so arranged that the pupil who masters them will have no difficulty in obtaining a *First Grade* Certificate from any County Superintendent.

By the end of the century state regulations had somewhat stiffened and an examination was required of those applying to teach. But by this time Sarah Dickey had added a fourth year to the Normal Course, and the catalogue assures any holder of a Certificate of Graduation from the course that she will have "no difficulty in obtaining a *First Grade Certificate* in any County Examination." These were no idle boasts. Teachers trained at Mount Hermon were in demand and the Certificates of Graduation from the Normal Course, treasured possessions.

The writer saw one of these certificates framed and hung in a prominent place in the home of a well-to-do widow whose maid had also attended Mount Hermon. Though friendly and glad to talk about her seminary days, the owner apparently thought too much of her certificate to allow it to be borrowed for photographing. It was an elegant affair in the best diploma tradition of the day. In the center of the large semicircle formed by the name of the Seminary was a picture of the seminary buildings. On either side were two parts of a verse from Proverbs, *A woman that feareth the Lord,* and *She shall be praised.* Prov. XXXI, 30. Then came the text:

This certifies that Emma E. J. Burrus has completed the Normal Course of study at Mount Hermon Seminary, and by her Attainments and Correct Deportment is entitled to this Certificate.
Given at Clinton, Mississippi, this 15th day of May, One Thousand and Eight Hundred and Ninety-five.

On one side of the circular seal at the bottom were the signatures of the president and secretary of the Board of Trustees, George Whitfield and N. W. Cabiness. On the other side were the signatures of Sarah Dickey as principal and those of three teachers. Anyone who has seen a Mount Holyoke Seminary diploma will recognize the model.

These certificates were as highly prized as any diploma; in effect they really were diplomas and so considered. The community looked on the Normal Course as the heart of Mount Hermon, and rightly so. There was no lack of students although numbers fluctuated erratically from year to year. One year seventy were enrolled. Yet up to the time of Sarah Dickey's death, of the hundreds who had begun the Normal Course, only thirty-seven had finished it and received the coveted certificates. For the first thirteen years of the Seminary no student completed the work. The accompanying table tells the story. It begins with 1889 when the first students graduated from the Normal Course. That is also the year of Julia Brown's graduation from the Advanced Course.

NUMBER OF GRADUATES FROM THE NORMAL COURSE
AND YEAR OF GRADUATION

1889............4	1893............2	1897............9	1901............6
1890............1	1894............0	1898............0	1902............0
1891............3	1895............1	1899............6	1903............0
1892............0	1896............2	1900............0	1904............3

This curious pattern of ups and downs makes little sense unless perhaps it reflects the financial condition of the families involved, as well it may. A snail-like, uneven pace of advancement marks all Negro education in the South at the time. Fisk University from 1875 to 1883 graduated only thirty-two among the thousands who had attended. Tougaloo University, in the same county as Mount Hermon, though it had a four-year head start and for some years received state money for its work in teacher training, did not graduate its first college class until 1901.

The low economic condition of the average southern Negro that kept so many students from graduating explains the way fees were handled at Mount Hermon and elsewhere. They were on a monthly instead of a term or year basis and had to be "paid promptly in advance," evidence of how little ready money the Negro had. Some students could attend for only a month or so at a time. Yet the fees were modest; they included board, tuition, fuel and lights and, unlike those of schools today, showed no tendency to spiral. It is possible to translate them into our more familiar yearly terms, for we know that Mount Hermon always opened the first week in October and closed the third week in May with a five day vacation at Christmas and, in later years, another five days in the spring. Four weeks, the catalogues tell us, constitute a school month. In the eighties the fee for the year was $68.00, but by the middle nineties it had been reduced, and for the year 1901-02 it was $53.00. The only other case of reduction of school fees that the writer knows of was at Mount Holyoke Seminary in its first years. When that seminary opened in 1837, the charge for room, board and tuition, exclusive of heat and light for the students' rooms, was $64.00. Mary Lyon was able to reduce it for the second year to $60.00 and it was kept at that figure for sixteen years! The Mount Hermon reductions, however, were not due to better management or cheaper prices. From the beginning Sarah Dickey had sailed as close to the wind as possible. Their cause lay rather in the worsening economic condition of the Negro and perhaps a little to the blunting of the edge of his desire for education since his early belief that it would open doors to him had not been justified.

Two other factors that help explain the slow and uneven development of the academic work at Mount Hermon are the rapid faculty turnover with consequent loss in continuity of instruction and the poor preparation of some of the teachers. That Sarah Dickey could not pick and choose her faculty but had to take what she could get was a serious handicap, for the quality of any school depends in large part on the quality of its faculty — on the preparation of its members, their teaching ability and their dedication to their work. At Mount Hermon there could have been little question about dedication. Only those moved by the need and able to help would have faced the long journey (no Southerner would teach in a Negro school), the poor and uncertain pay and the certain social ostracism. These drawbacks throw light on the rapid turnover. Also missionary zeal, unfortunately for Mount Hermon, is no guarantee of sound preparation and teaching skill. It is probably no coincidence that the only two Mount Holyoke graduates to teach at Mount Hermon taught there, the one for the year '87-'88 and the other for that of '88-'89, the two years in which Julia Brown took the Advanced Course and received the seminary diploma. They were also the years when the first students, four of them, finished the Normal Course and received the first certificates of graduation from it.

Except for one group, very little is known of the many teachers who came and went in rapid succession. Two of them in the early eighties did yeoman service in preparing a leaflet for Sarah Dickey's use in introducing herself and her school to possible donors. They also tried to raise money for Mount Hermon when they returned to their native Massachusetts. For the elementary work, however, the Seminary was not entirely dependent on teachers from away. In the catalogues, after the names of the teachers comes the caption "Assistant pupil teachers." This use of the older and better pupils to help with the younger ones was a regular feature of Mount Hermon and gave valuable practice to those chosen.

In the 1882-'83 catalogue there is yet another category, one reminiscent of Mount Holyoke, that of Lecturers. Then follow the names of Rev. Walter Hillman, president of her Board of Trustees, who, as we know, had been president of Mississippi College and whose own school he was slowly raising to college status; Rev. George Whitfield, president of Mississippi College; and Rev. Stanley Pope, recently retired president of Tougaloo University, living at the time in Clinton. These experienced educators had much to give Mount Hermon and added to its prestige. Sarah Dickey also made use of visitors to the school. Rev. W. J. Shuey's report of a three day visit to Mount Hermon in 1881 mentions a lecture on Africa that he gave there.

The group of teachers that we do know something about is that of Sarah Dickey's relatives. The use of them as a source of teacher supply came about naturally. She had gone North at the time of her beloved sister's death and in her warm-hearted

way had offered a home to her sister's daughters, Maud and
Olive Mather, and to an elderly aunt, Miss Adaline Taylor.
Once back at Mount Hermon she incorporated all three into the
school. Maud, the older niece, was the little girl who had been
so eager to go to the barbecue on the day of the terrible Clinton
riot. Now in her early twenties, she took an active part in the
work of the school. She taught third and fourth grade, some
subjects in the Normal Course, and, showing general com-
petence, she was soon put in charge of the cooking and housework. Small wonder that she stayed only a few years!

Olive, in her teens, entered the Normal Course as a student
and helped with the first and second graders. There was not
yet a school segregation law in the state. The children of two
white families connected with Mount Hermon also went to
school there. In 1891 when Olive finished the Normal Course,
her aunt took her to Dr. Hillman's school to be prepared for
entrance to Lake Erie Seminary in Ohio. It was much nearer than
Mount Holyoke. Its principal had been one of Sarah Dickey's
teachers at Mount Holyoke, and it provided much the same sort
of training, a training she wanted her niece to have in order to
help her at Mount Hermon. All went according to plan. Olive
graduated from Lake Erie in 1898 and returned to assist her
aunt at Mount Hermon. At Lake Erie she had been editor of
the literary magazine and president of the Debating Society, but
music was her greatest interest and her special gift. In a letter
Sarah Dickey wrote early in 1900 she said of her niece that
though she was not in the best of health she was doing such
good work that she [Miss Dickey] did not know how she could
get along without her. By 1901 Olive Mather appears in the
catalogue not only as teacher of vocal and instrumental music
but also as associate principal and matron, the two positions
best calculated to give her an understanding of the problems
and management of the school. Was she being groomed to
succeed her aunt?

If so, it was in vain. The very next year her name disappears
from the catalogue. If Olive Mather's marriage was a disappointment to her aunt, no hint of it appears. It may not have

been a disappointment, for Sarah Dickey loved her niece and would have wanted whatever was best for her. She was sure that the Lord, who had brought Mount Hermon into being, would continue to take care of it. "God's own work," she called it.

So Olive was married at Mount Hermon where Mary Caldwell had been married and Willette Campbell and others brought up by Sarah Dickey. Rev. George Whitfield, now president of Mount Hermon's Board of Trustees, conducted the marriage service. The bridegroom, Claude Saum, was a young lawyer Olive had met while visiting a Lake Erie friend. After the wedding he took her to his Illinois home. Two years later they were called back when Sarah Dickey was on her deathbed. They were there when she made her will and appointed her nephew-in-law her executor. So after her death the Saums stayed on, he to settle the estate and Olive to fill out as acting principal the remaining three-and-a-half months of the school year. Then they left for the North, settling in Watseka, Illinois, and had no further dealings with or, apparently, interest in Mount Hermon.

It is hard to get a clear image of Olive Mather Saum, the niece so carefully cared for and dearly loved. A Clinton citizen spoke of "Miss Dickey's beautiful niece." Mrs. Coats who, though older, had graduated in the same Normal class with her, said that Olive was a very pretty girl with whom she had many good times. The comments of those who came later and knew her only as a teacher indicate in one way or another only that "she wasn't one bit like Miss Dickey." Certainly the increased emphasis on music in the later years of the Seminary was due to her and a real contribution to Mount Hermon.

Very different was the response to inquiries about Sarah Dickey's aunt, Miss Adaline Taylor. "Miss Adaline was old and bent, but we-all thought a heap of her" was a characterization repeated in different ways. A very fine needlewoman herself, she set high standards for the girls in her sewing classes. In a picture of the class of 1897 (p. 117) we see the nine young women in becoming dark suits and white blouses, mortar

Above: Mount Hermon Seminary, Main Building and East Wing
Below: The Class of 1897

boards on their heads made of the same material as the suits. These "graduating gowns," a caption under the picture explained, were "made by themselves at a cost of a trifle less than $2.00 each." Sarah Dickey gave her aunt the room behind hers, the room with the shared connecting closet and washing arrangements that Mary Caldwell had had as a child. A gentle, efficient, friendly sort of person, "Miss Adaline," in spite of her age, assumed more and more responsibility as time went on. What a comfort it must have been to Sarah Dickey to have her mother's sister with her!

Another relative, who in her brief stay of two years made a considerable impression on her students, was a cousin, Margaret Dickey. Those who had studied under her talked about how much they learned. "A extra fine teacher," they said. A Democrat, she had once made it possible for Claude Inge to hear William Jennings Bryan speak in Jackson on the condition that he was not to tell staunch Republican Miss Dickey she had done so.

A nephew, Charles Surface, turned up occasionally, not to help with the school, but to be helped. He seems to have been not very successful in business and his aunt at the time of her death was doing all she could to aid him. In her will she writes, "I desire that my nephew's note which I hold shall be cancelled and delivered to him — the amount of which has been paid in interest. (the amount being $1,000.00) and the nephew's name being C. F. Surface." If the interest on the thousand dollars had already amounted to a thousand, she must have lent the money some years earlier. That she was especially concerned for his welfare is shown further in the will. Her two largest bequests to individuals are to her niece Olive Mather Saum, and her nephew, Charles F. Surface — $1,000.00 to each. The relatives who had been so sure that Sarah Dickey was wasting money and time in trying to get more than a common school education gladly accepted the fact of her success and her willingness to help their children when she could. Some of the benefits were reciprocal; those who taught did good work at Mount Hermon.

If only there had been a farmer in her family to help her run the farm! It was a necessary part of Mount Hermon, for the table was largely supplied by it. In the early years a big Negro family was housed in the Seminary, the father and boys working the farm and caring for the stock, the wife helping with the cooking. Toward the end Sarah Dickey made use of white "superintendents." The Rev. John S. Brown was such a one; his wife taught the first four grades and their three children attended school at Mount Hermon. But for the most part she got along with local help. Many of the men who as boys had gone to school at Mount Hermon had worked on the farm either as boys or later. One of them remarked that the farm didn't amount to much because Miss Dickey's trips North came at a time when the work needed supervision. However, in spite of difficulties, the farm seems always to have supplied the table with food that the boarding pupils pronounced "very good."

Whatever reservations we may have about the teachers and teaching at Mount Hermon, it is certain that the recipients of that education had no doubts about its value. And compared with anything else within their reach they were right in their estimate. Consequently the school drew students from an increasingly wide geographic area in the state and even a few from Arkansas and Louisiana. One catalogue lists students from nine Mississippi counties extending all the way from southeastern Jackson County on the Gulf of Mexico to northwestern Bolivar County in the rich Delta region.

But numbers, as always, brought problems. Students from away must be housed and fed. Sarah Dickey has been described by some of her former pupils as "always building." Sometimes it would be just an extra room here or two rooms there, perhaps to house some old woman she was befriending; more often it was an enlargement for the school itself. As early as 1880 or 1881 she added the large four-story wing to the main house, the east wing (p. 117). The chapel was there, and below it. for the building was on a slope, were the kitchen and dining room. On the floors above the chapel were dormitory rooms. The catalogue for 1882-'83 says that when these apartments

(her word) are finished sixty boarding students can be accommodated. The laundry, built a little later, was a three-story
frame structure with a basement that opened on the slope and
served for the primary grades. On the first floor was what a
former student described as "a fine arrangement of wooden tubs
with stoppers." A school room and the "pressing room" were
on the floor above. The top floor contained more dormitory
rooms. Another building, put up still later, was the small boys'
dormitory. Barn and woodshed received additions too, for
Mount Hermon provided its own milk and butter, eggs, chickens and turkeys. Whenever any building was going on, Sarah
Dickey was there, climbing up and down ladders, keeping watch
over every detail. No slipshod work was allowed, and repairs
were kept up, a splendid training for the men and boys who
worked under her.

One may well ask where Sarah Dickey could have raised the
money for these buildings, for the teachers' salaries and for the
general maintenance of the school. When Mount Hermon
opened on that October day in 1875, the second three thousand
dollars for the property was still to be raised — and within a
limited time. At first there was no philanthropic foundation to
which Sarah Dickey might make application for aid. (The Pea-
body Fund gave only to state normal schools.) It had taken her
over two years of almost constant endeavor to raise the first
three thousand, and the resources of some of her donors were
exhausted. She could not expect much from the Mississippi
Negroes who had given most of the first thousand. Their economic condition was steadily deteriorating. Then over and
above this indebtedness of three thousand, running expenses had
to be met and more equipment bought for school and farm.
There was no one on her biracial Board of Trustees who could
help financially; there was no church group or any other group
to undertake fund-raising. Unofficially her own church, the
United Brethren, helped Mount Hermon in many ways through
the years just as the Congregational church had stood by Mount
Holyoke in its early days. But neither church was responsible
for the necessary money-raising.

What Sarah Dickey did have, however, was her all-sustaining conviction that God had called her to this particular task and so if she faithfully did all that was within her power, she could leave the results to Him. *All that was within her power* — how much that clause covered! For carrying out her assignment she had two great resources, an alert mind and an indomitable spirit that could and did rise above discouragements and failures. She drove herself unmercifully. There is a rare admission of weariness in a plea for more support written the summer of 1886.

And, oh; what would not this tired mind and frame give for one brief week of entire rest from work and care. But just now the work seems to be rushing upon us like a great avalanche, and the demands are greater than ever. Money, buildings, furniture, and repairs and improvements, in doors and out, up stairs and down, are wanted.

No wonder she was bone-weary, for by 1886 she had already accomplished what borders on the miraculous. She had paid, to the surprise and possible disappointment of the former owners, the second three thousand when it became due in 1878. She had raised an additional nine thousand dollars which she had put into buildings and furniture, thereby increasing the value of the Mount Hermon property. In 1878 a committee of the United Brethren, considering lending money on the property, had appraised it at five thousand though they knew it had been bought five years earlier for six. Yet by 1886 in the Slater Fund report the property is said to be "worth about $20,000."

We ask again, how had Sarah Dickey, single-handed, brought about this change? Where did the money come from? It came from various sources — from borrowing, from personal solicitation, for a few years from the Slater Fund, and from publicity efforts. As for borrowing, it is difficult for a layman to make his way through the jungle of mortgages, liens, and deeds of trust that appear in the abstract of title for the Mount Hermon property. Sarah Dickey would pay an indebtedness when it came due by incurring another. For instance, in a report made to the United Brethren's Board of Missions by the committee referred to above, the following appears after a description of the property:

The only incumbrance on the property is a trust-deed for $1,444, which is now due and demanded.

Miss S. A. Dickey asks this Board to loan her out of its permanent fund the sum of $1,500, to bear interest at the rate of eight per cent per annum, with which to cancel this debt of trust, which loan is to be secured by a deed of trust on the institution. . . .

The report goes on to recommend the loan and is signed by the three committee members headed by Rev. W. J. Shuey. The recommendation was accepted. This 1878 transaction marks the beginning of W. J. Shuey's long and helpful friendship with Mount Hermon and its founder. It is not necessary, even were it possible, to follow the many borrowings from banks, from church organizations and from various individuals — J. D. Coleman, for instance, who kept the general store in Clinton and taught at Mississippi College, or A. B. Simpson of New York City and the Christian Alliance. Sarah Dickey was never out of debt, but never worried by the fact. Clearly her credit was good and she knew how to make use of it. She was interested in real estate, too, and occasionally took proffered property in lieu of a student's fees. A good business woman herself, she had good advisers in her three lawyer friends, two of them colored and one white. Her frequent borrowings were for the purpose of meeting some special need; most of the money for running expenses came from personal solicitation.

That is why she had to make such long, tiring trips North. She would be away from one to three months every year. She usually went first to Mount Holyoke, trying to arrive for the commencement season at which she became a familiar and welcome figure. Besides money and goodwill, she collected clothing. Shipped South in barrels, it was mended, cleaned and sold to Clinton Negroes at modest prices. She was against hand-outs in any form.

The other place where she always stopped on these trips was Dayton, Ohio. She never failed to find spiritual refreshment from her dearly loved church, as well as material aid. Sometimes she stayed with the Shueys, discussing Mount Hermon affairs with the friend whose judgment she valued. And in Dayton were also some of her most generous contributors.

She needed no introduction to these two places, but when she went to a town where she was not known she usually sent ahead to some minister there the four-page leaflet, mentioned earlier, introducing her and Mount Hermon. It served its purpose well, for when she presented herself and perhaps asked for hospitality while she approached possible donors in the town, she usually found a ready welcome. Her host often gave her letters of introduction to key people in the town and to other ministers. This way of going about her task explains the relatively small area in which she worked. She would be passed on from one well-wishing minister to another.

That the introductory leaflet proved such an open sesame for her is not strange. Prepared by two of her teachers in 1880 it was later reprinted and brought up to date. On the first page is a brief account of Mount Hermon and its need. The two inner pages contain "Commendations" from such people as Noah Porter, president of Yale University; the principal and associate principals of Mount Holyoke Seminary; the principal of Lake Erie Seminary; the general agent of the American Missionary Association; a Richmond, Indiana, banker; the president of the Columbus, Ohio, Rolling Mill Company; together with a liberal sprinkling of clergymen and professors — an impressive list and impressive testimonials. Here is what Rev. N. G. Clarke, D.D., secretary of the Missionary Bureau in Boston wrote:

> Having known Miss Dickey at Mt. Holyoke Seminary and her work in the South, I am glad to commend her and her cause to all who are interested in the moral elevation of the colored people — especially of colored women. Miss Dickey is a woman of *rare devotion,* and of the *loftiest purpose* — a sort of Mary Lyon for Mississippi.

On the fourth page is a long list of names and addresses of "Other Personal Friends and Donors," a list that starts off with the name of General John Eaton, Commissioner of Education, Washington, D.C. These names come from those who had known Sarah Dickey at the various periods of her life going back to her Vicksburg days. Among those from her later life in Mississippi is that of the Superintendent of Public Education for the state.

Valuable as this leaflet was in establishing Sarah Dickey's claim to the attention of men and women of good will, it did not take the place of personal interviews. There was evidently something about her that aroused interest and loosened purse strings. Her drive, her accurate knowledge of conditions in the South and her obvious common sense all played a part in securing each year enough or almost enough to cover salaries, food, repairs, and other expenses involved in running a growing school. Yet at best it was a hand-to-mouth existence that promised no security for the future. The plea in the 1880 leaflet that the school "be at once *endowed,* as the work ABSOLUTELY DEMANDS" had brought no endowment. Extra money all went into necessary building. But as far as running expenses went, the pressure was mercifully lessened in 1884 and for seven years after by an annual grant of a thousand dollars from the recently established John F. Slater Fund for the Education of Freedmen. At the same time pressure for raising an endowment was increased as it became evident that continuance of the grant depended on assurance of permanence either by securing an endowment or by affiliation with some established institution.

The John F. Slater Fund had been set up in 1882 by John F. Slater, a Connecticut cotton textile manufacturer who had inherited the business from his uncle, Samuel Slater, an Englishman. The latter, in partnership with Moses Brown, a Rhode Island Quaker, started the cotton textile industry in this country. Ironically, as has been pointed out, the two things that fastened the institution of slavery on the South were the application of power-driven machinery (designed by Samuel Slater from his memory of such machinery in England and financed by Moses Brown) to the spinning of cotton yarn and the invention two years later by Eli Whitney of the cotton gin. Was it some sense of responsibility that caused the nephew, who had further developed the New England mills and prospered greatly, to turn his attention to the situation in the South? He himself puts it also on patriotic grounds, saying that while he felt compassion for the freedmen whose ignorance was due to no fault of their own, he was likewise concerned for the safety of his country if so large a block of citizens lacked education. Then, having chosen a Board of Trustees to administer the fund he proposed to set up, he explained his purpose more fully as follows:

The general object which I desire to have exclusively pursued is the uplifting of the lately emancipated population of the Southern States and their posterity, by conferring on them the blessings of Christian education. The disabilities formerly suffered by these people, and their singular patience and fidelity in the great crisis of the nation, establish a just claim on the sympathy and good will of humane and patriotic men.

His plan was to assist schools already in operation rather than to establish new ones.

The trustees John F. Slater chose were a distinguished group. Rutherford B. Hayes, his term as President of the United States just over, became the Board's first president. They began their work by appointing a prominent Southern clergyman, Rev. Atticus C. Haygood, as their agent to visit and investigate all schools that applied for aid and on the basis of what he found make recommendations each year to the Board at its annual meeting.

As soon as Sarah Dickey heard of this fund, she made application, and Dr. Haygood visited Mount Hermon during the first year of the Fund's operation, 1883-'84. He was so much impressed by the work being done there that he recommended an appropriation of one thousand dollars for the next year. Part of his assignment was to check each year on the schools receiving grants, find out just how the money had been spent, note changes and decide whether the grant should be renewed or not. He continued his recommendation of Mount Hermon as long as he was agent in spite of the fact that the trustees had adopted a resolution that "no money be appropriated to institutions that are not, with good reason, believed to be on a permanent basis." That the grant lasted as long as it did is another illustration of the confidence that Sarah Dickey inspired. Given time she would surely raise the needed amount. Or it may be that he deliberately disregarded the resolution. Before he had started in on the work, he had visited John F.

Slater to get his ideas at first hand, and he may have thought that Mount Hermon was the sort of school Mr. Slater would approve of. The trustees' point of view is equally understandable. Why invest in something that has an uncertain future?

In his first report Dr. Haygood called Mount Hermon Seminary "one of the best of its class" and went on to say that "with larger resources, richly deserved, much more might be done." These yearly reports, in addition to providing the vital statistics about the schools and itemized accounts as to how the grants had been spent, include comments like the above. The report for 1889-'90 records that four thousand dollars worth of improvements had been added to Mount Hermon within the year. The attendance figures given in these reports show the only regular curve in the history of Mount Hermon. They rise progressively from 150 in 1885 to 254 in 1891. There was an increase in the number of teachers as well.

In 1891 Dr. Haygood resigned as agent of the Slater Fund to beçome bishop of the Southern Methodist Episcopal Church. Sarah Dickey had already seen the handwriting on the wall. With no prospect of an endowment in the foreseeable future, she decided that the only way to provide permanence for Mount Hermon and continuance of the Slater grant would be to offer the school to the Mission Board of the United Brethren or to the American Missionary Association. She put the situation before her trustees. They raised no objection and were entirely willing to transfer their ownership to any organization able and willing to give Mount Hermon the stability it so much needed and free Miss Dickey from the strain she had been under.

Unfortunately in 1890 when the offer was first made to the United Brethren, there had recently been a split in the church. It was not a time for taking on any new projects. The minutes of the Executive Committee of the United Brethren Board of Missions for March 31, 1890 read:

Whereas Miss Dickey of Mt. Hermon Seminary at Mt. [*sic*] Clinton, Miss. has written that she desires to dispose of her seminary either to U.B. Church or to American Missionary Assoc. the officers are instructed to write her at once and say that we as a society cannot purchase

her institution, and that we would be glad to receive our money invested
there as soon as possible.

Needless to say, Rev. W. J. Shuey was no longer on the committee. The next year Sarah Dickey appears in person, and a
more friendly minute is penned under the date of June 30, 1891.

Miss Dickey of Mississippi came in and asked that the Board take the
work she has on hand in her Seminary for girls near Clinton, Miss. The
Com. heard her with deep interest and appreciate highly, her long self
sacrificing work almost alone in the midst of great opposition and general indifference, but are not prepared today to give any encouragement
because we have no money and it is so remote from our other work.

Then Sarah Dickey turned to the American Missionary Association. Dr. Frank Woodworth, president of Tougaloo, was
a good friend of hers and an admirer of the work she was doing,
but the officers of the Association in New York were not interested. They already had one school, Tougaloo, in the area and
that was enough.

Hence when the blow fell, as fall it did after Dr. Haygood's
resignation took effect and Mount Hermon had received a reduced farewell grant of $666.66 for 1892 before being dropped
from the Slater list, Sarah Dickey took up again the task of
soliciting full support for Mount Hermon.

In one of Dr. Haygood's reports to the trustees of the Slater
Fund he had quoted from a letter in which Sarah Dickey had
written, "We cannot estimate how much we are indebted to
the trustees of the Slater Fund. Without their aid we see no
way to keep the work up." Yet when that aid was withdrawn,
Sarah Dickey did "keep the work up" without faltering and
without lament. She wrote later and in another connection:

I asked God when I started this work to keep me sweet; never to let
me become soured, or let me feel hard toward anyone because he or
she did not give to me. And I thank Him that He has done what I
asked of Him.

Uncomplainingly she shouldered the whole of the load once
more. She put her good mind, so fertile in producing ideas for
developing Mount Hermon, on ways to reach a wider public
and secure the long talked about and increasingly necessary

endowment. She knew that time was running out. Personal
interviews were by their nature restricted in number and geographical range. The loss of help from the Slater Fund em-
phasized the need for some large-scale money-raising campaign.

In preparation for such a campaign she drew up a statement
of Mount Hermon's minimum needs: $35,000 as endowment
for teachers' salaries, $15,000 for building and equipment, and
$3,000 for the construction of an "excellent" cotton gin and
corn grinder. The operation of the machinery, she estimated,
should give Mount Hermon from six to seven hundred dollars
additional yearly income. It would also provide employment
under good working conditions for needy Clinton Negroes.

To publicize these needs she turned first to those with whom
she already had a connection, the Mount Holyoke alumnae.
These women were pretty well scattered over the country, holding positions of influence as teachers and wives. While few of
them could give much in their own right, they could be centers
of information in their communities and so reach the much
needed wider public. She drafted and had printed a letter to be
sent to each alumna. It began by saying that she knew that

ever since the burning of the building [the capacious old main build-
ing] of our beloved alma mater, the members of the Alumnae Association have been straining every nerve to keep the Institution in her
proper place, foremost of women [*sic*] colleges. [She has] refrained
from bringing before many of them this worthy child Seminary. . . .
[But now she feels that] the time has come when the blessed Master
would be pleased to have the dear members of the Alumnae Association
know of this work and of its needs. . . .

She goes on to explain those needs ending her plea for help,
"Yours in bonds of Mt. Holyoke," and signs her name. She
sent this to a classmate who happened to be secretary of the
Mount Holyoke Alumnae Association at the time and so in a
position to carry out the project if the Association and the
College agreed to it. One is sorry but not surprised that neither
body thought it advisable to circularize the alumnae. After all,
other Mount Holyoke women were engaged in other needy and
worthy causes the world over. Consequently no endowment,
building fund or cotton gin materialized from this effort.

She analyzes her situation in the following way preparatory to introducing another plan:

> Among the many hindrances I meet with is this one — that I have no way of bringing my work before the people except to go to them in person, which makes the work very hard for me. And as many of my old contributors have passed away, I find it very difficult, by going in person, to find new ones to take their places. . . . Because this work is not sectarian I cannot get it before the public through the denominational periodicals [actually her own church paper, *The Religious Telescope*, was generous with its space]; nor through the churches, which are already burdened with good works in their own denominations. So now I am going to try a new plan, and if this is not sufficient I shall try something else —whatever may be suggested.

The "new plan" was a publication aimed not only to introduce Mount Hermon to the longed-for wider public but also to keep that public in touch with it. Only two numbers of *The Dew of Hermon,* as the little paper was called, appeared, the first dated September 1900 and the second, July 1901. The Rev. John S. Brown was editor of the first. It was little more than a leaflet, but the second, with Sarah A. Dickey as "Editor and Publisher," is twelve pages long and illustrated. The intention of quarterly publication is announced and the terms given. The price of a year's subscription is twenty-five cents, but subscriptions to "clubs" of six, twenty-five, fifty and a hundred are offered at reduced rates. Since only two numbers appeared it would seem that none of the "clubs" so hopefully suggested was ever formed nor is there evidence that any large contributions resulted.

Yet this second number is both informative and appealing. The first of three full-page illustrations is a picture of the Seminary on its wooded knoll, the next is of the class of 1897 in the neat suits they made for their graduation, and the last is of the class of 1901 in the more conventional but becoming white commencement dresses they too had made. On next to the last page are two strong testimonials, one headed "What the President of Mount Holyoke College says" and the other "From a Colored Presiding Elder of the M. E. Church." On the last page are the names of the trustees; the names of the six teachers follow with the subjects they taught, beginning with Miss Sarah A. Dickey, Principal, Bible and Bible Studies. Rev. J. S. Brown is listed as superintendent.

The one article, entitled "Prospectus," occupies the main part of the little paper and is signed "Humbly yours for God and Humanity, Sarah A. Dickey." It begins by telling briefly the things in her life that had led her to the work she was doing, of her struggle for an education, of Vicksburg and her dream, of how she got to Mount Holyoke, of her decision to give up the idea of Africa and devote her life to Negro education in the South, of the difficulties she encountered in starting her school, of its development and needs, and ends with a plea for help in continuing the important work. Her terse factual description of Mount Hermon is worth quoting; it shows the sort of people she hoped to interest.

> Mt. Hermon Seminary is a chartered institution, has an incorporated Board of Trustees, is well established; has eighty-two girls in school and has had over twenty conversions in this year. It is an industrial school, established and carried on as nearly on the plan of the Mt. Holyoke Seminary, in Massachusetts, as the circumstances would allow.

This attempt to enlist a wider circle of contributors, eloquent and moving as some of it is, failed to catch the eye of anyone able and willing to do for Mount Hermon what John D. Rockefeller and his wife, Laura Spelman Rockefeller, did for the struggling Atlanta Baptist Female Seminary that later became known, first as Spelman Seminary and then in 1924 as Spelman College. After all, most wealthy philanthropists belonged, as did Rockefeller, to a church that supported work of its own for Negroes in the South. A non-sectarian enterprise had a more difficult task to find supporters. But as Sarah Dickey wrote:

> Although the churches are doing so much through their own Missionary Boards, yet there are large hearted individuals in all of them who will also help a work like this if they know about it. And outside of the churches are multitudes of the Abou ben Adhem sort, who love their fellowmen and love to help them.

Alas, no Abou ben Adhem appeared to warrant the continuance of the new quarterly! So here was another hopeful venture that did scarcely more than get off the ground, a venture into which Sarah Dickey must have put a great deal of time, effort, and money.

Yet she refused to be downcast. She was weary; the annual trips North had become increasingly burdensome; her rheumatic attacks were more frequent; she was losing by death some of her most generous contributors; her niece on whom she had counted had married and gone away. But her spirit was indomitable. Quoting again from *The Dew of Hermon,*

> As to this work Satan may just as well take his hands off. He now says: "You have got about to the end of all you can do." But I know he is a liar and always has been, and there is no truth in him. My blessed Master never put me in this work to be baffled or defeated by that evil one. He says: "Resist the devil and he will flee from you." And I know it is true.

So she continued her exhausting money-raising efforts. The flame of her faith burned steadily. She knew on the one hand that Mount Hermon was "God's own work," and on the other, that she was the instrument chosen to labor in its behalf. She sometimes expresses in her letters thankfulness in having been so "honored." Her spirit was upheld by this sense of divine commission.

8.   The Wider Community

VARIED AND insistent as were the demands that Mount Hermon made upon its founder, they by no means covered the scope of Sarah Dickey's activities. In a letter she wrote in 1901 for her class round robin, she says, "My work . . . does not end within the walls of Mt. Hermon Seminary. Fully half of the work my hand findeth to do cannot be reported in a school catalogue." Any need within her power to fill had claim on her. Just as we saw her adapt her Seminary for young women in such a way as to include the colored boys and girls of Clinton and elsewhere who otherwise would have had no schooling, so we see her dealing with a social problem much on the public mind today — old age. Not that she thought of it as a social problem. It was only a matter of individuals who needed a home and care; her reaction was that of a friend. The Negro cabins of the time were small and the Negro families large; there was plenty of room at Mount Hermon. Thus we find at Mount Hermon a number of old women, each living a separate, independent life. Some were able to help a little about the place, but most of them were beyond their working years. The one to whom Sarah Dickey was personally devoted had worked at Charles Caldwell's when Sarah Dickey lived there. She was known as Granny Sukey-Bukey, a remarkable old woman of Creole or Indian extraction whose memory went far back into her slave days. She was immensely old though not the "bout hundred forty" that she herself claimed. Her good judgment and salty common sense, much enjoyed by Sarah Dickey, stayed with her to the end. Her last years were happy ones in the little cabin built for her on the grounds. At her funeral, attended by the entire school, the presiding minister firmly rebuked the little boys who smiled at her funny name, for Sukey-Bukey was all the name she seems ever to have had. She was buried in the graveyard on the grounds.

Granny Sukey-Bukey was the only one of the old women who had been a personal friend of their benefactress. The others came through this person and that. One was Aunt Margaret, who was able to do a little work for her keep. She was an aunt of one of the students. Another, Aunt Martha, was Allen Putnam's grandmother. Allen Putnam had finished the elementary work and the first year of the Normal Course. He was especially devoted to Sarah Dickey and the school. Yet another old woman, the already mentioned Aunt Cheney, was a vagrant no one seemed to know anything about. She is remembered because in order to take care of her when she was ill, Sarah Dickey gave the village children that unexpected holiday. And there were others, a changing group of elderly waifs whose last days were spent in Mount Hermon's friendly environment.

Other needs of the Negro community Sarah Dickey was quick to see. She often stood between the Negroes and any white man unscrupulous enough to take advantage of the ignorance and shiftless ways of many of them. For instance, when Negroes took their cotton to the cotton market in Bolton, they were given receipts. Unfamiliar with such a practice and having no place to keep stray pieces of paper, as the receipts seemed to some of them, the Negroes often lost their receipts before pay day came round, a mischance that certain cotton traders counted on and did not hesitate to profit by. The Negro would lose his year's work. When Negroes Sarah Dickey knew went to Bolton for their pay, she often found occasion to go there too. Her presence assured fair treatment; her word that the cotton had been raised and delivered was accepted without dispute.

There were other sharp practices, too, about which Sarah Dickey heard and did what she could to correct, or at least to mitigate. A Northerner living in Edwards lent money to Negroes and was not above taking advantage of their ignorance, but never if the Negro had been recommended by Miss Dickey. Another way in which she felt the Negroes were sometimes exploited was on the plantations where many of them still lived, some of them in the same cabins they had occupied in slave days. Even though they might not be sharecroppers but worked elsewhere, they were still more or less at the mercy of the man on whose land they lived. She was also concerned bcause their children usually lived too far away from school to get any sort of an education. One man told me that because he grew up on a distant plantation, he was able to go to school in such small scraps, just a day here and there, that he never got beyond first grade. He was the one who said that on Sunday the whole family always drove to Mount Hermon for Sunday school and church, the one day that gave interest and meaning to their lives.

Sarah Dickey, putting her good mind on the problem of these plantation Negroes, came up with an idea. She invited those she thought would be most interested to meet with her one evening at Mount Hermon. She told them that she was willing to borrow money to buy a 120 acre piece of land that lay between the railroad station and Mount Hermon. She had already found out that the owner of the land, the son-in-law of Mr. Rice from whom Mount Hermon had been bought, would sell it to her, and the price. She would buy it and have it surveyed into lots provided, she told her spellbound audience, that a sufficient number of them cared enough for the education of their children and their own independence to find ways of earning money to pay for a lot and to build a house on it. Always Sarah Dickey expected the Negro to do his share. He must learn to stand on his own feet. She knew that the long years of servitude had conditioned him to hand-outs. She gave nothing away except to the old, the ill and the helpless. Now she was offering these men an opportunity to become independent home owners.

The Negroes gathered there that evening listened entranced, hardly daring to believe in the prospect she held forth. They knew that she could borrow the amount of money needed for this venture. Her credit was good and she was used to borrowing money. They were proud of this ability as well as of other evidences of her standing in the white community. One of them delightedly repeated a conversation overheard at the Merchants Bank. It went something like this: Miss Dickey to the cashier, "Mr. Neal, I want to borrow five hundred dollars. How long will it take to arrange the loan?" "I'll give it to you right now, Miss Sarah," the cashier had replied and began counting out the money. There would be no trouble about her ability to borrow the money, but how could they get enough to buy and build?

At twenty dollars an acre, the price she set, the money would be hard to come by. And building a house on the land would cost considerably more even for those who could do the work themselves. She did not minimize the difficulties, but she did suggest that those interested might meet with her at Mount Hermon weekly to discuss ways and means until the project was well started. The suggestion was welcomed and a group of prospective home owners formed. A by-product of these meetings was the sense of community fellowship that developed. It was decided to reserve the first lot as site for a community church and, in 1898, the Holy Ghost Baptist church was built on it. (It was one of the thirty-eight Mississippi churches burned in 1964.) Sarah Dickey organized the boys of the interested families into a squad for cutting and selling cordwood to help pay for their parents' lots. She also lent money to a few without charging interest (the regular interest rate at that time was 10%) and even built two or three houses which she sold to the lot owners on the installment plan. I was told by a white resident that she lost on some of these ventures. Very possibly she did lose, but she certainly had no regrets, for the project accomplished the purpose for which it was intended. Dickeyville, as that section is still called on the Clinton survey map, stands as a memorial to her.

Sarah Dickey made very sure that her activities were well within the Mississippi law, always consulting one or more of her three special lawyer friends. She got help of other kinds from a townsman who combined teaching mathematics at Mississippi College with running a store. Admiring her greatly, he helped her with accounts and loaned her money. His was a strange history. As a young man he had fled Georgia, his native state, to avoid punishment for killing a boy. Reaching Mississippi, he established himself in Clinton, obtained a teaching position in the Baptist college there and married the local judge's daughter — all this in spite of the fact that everyone seems to have known what he had done.

From these many activities and relationships, it is clear that the attitude of the white community to Sarah Dickey had greatly altered from the days when she had been shunned, hooted at and threatened. The change had come slowly, but by 1889 she could write in her class letter for '69's round robin:

One grand point gained I must mention. One of the good things which I so much longed to do in this vicinity was to live down the prejudice which the southern people had against the northern people who came down to teach the colored. In the depths of humility and gratitude, I can say that has been done, completely done; all the credit, honor and praise, I give to the Dear Lord, in whose hands I am.

When one remembers that in 1871 on her arrival at Clinton no white family would take her in, that the women in church would not sit in the same pew with her, and that the college boys made a practice of annoying and insulting her on the street, one realizes what a miracle was wrought by the work she was doing and by her courageous, friendly life. By the late eighties the college boys raised their hats when they passed her and gave her the whole of the two-plank sidewalk. She had also won the confidence of the leading people in the town — and their gratitude.

For little by little the town realized her value to it. The whole atmosphere of the Negro community had altered; it was more orderly and law-abiding. The village fathers sent her an official vote of thanks for her work for the colored girls and children. The alteration in her personal relations with the better element in the town is shown as early as 1886 when she worked with a group of Clinton women, many of them wives of the first citizens, in a prohibition campaign for the passage of a local option bill. Evidently her work was so outstanding that when the bill was passed she received a testimonial from some of the prominent men of the town for what she had done. Even in the always more conservative rural districts there was some modification, if we may judge by incidents such as the following. Traveling in the country with a Negro friend, she had spent the night in the crowded Negro quarters of a plantation where there was only one bed for the two of them. It was all their hostess, one of the servants, had to offer. The next morning the mistress of the "big house" happened to see them drive away and, recognizing Miss Dickey, called her servant to her to say that if ever Miss Dickey came again, she was to stay in the "big house" with her.

Apparently the white community had adjusted itself to the fact that Sarah Dickey lived with and treated Negroes exactly as she did white people. "She didn't know any difference between white and colored," one Negro said — surely the greatest compliment possible. It meant that she saw people as God must see them, each an individual and of value. But she did see that the Negroes, individually and collectively, had special need of help. She worked for them, as we have seen, in many ways that had little to do with her cherished dream of a second Mount Holyoke. Think of the old people she cared for, the children she raised, the education of the village boys and girls, her protection of Negro rights, her sale of clothing, Dickeyville, her land project. She felt amply repaid by the love and devotion that was hers. She knew the Negro's unswerving loyalty once his confidence was won. "If white folks had been mean to Miss Dickey, we sure would have riz up," one of them said.

We have these various glimpses of Sarah Dickey's life and work in Clinton and recognize her impact on the town. But of her life away from Clinton we know astonishingly little. During the years the writer was in Mississippi and interested in putting together details of her life, though she was told much about what Sarah Dickey did in the school and for the community, no one with whom she talked could remember hearing

Miss Dickey speak of her travels and personal experiences while out of the state or about the church to which she belonged. This is surprising. In her yearly trips North she must have seen and done much that would be of interest to her students. Her daily chapel talks, however, and her many other talks evidently dealt exclusively with the students' own needs and problems. One of her Mount Holyoke classmates refers to "Sarah's besetting sin, humility." Did that figure in this suppression of herself in her many talks? Or did she think that extending the students' horizon by glimpses of the world outside might make for discontent? She always tried to teach her students how to make the most of their own environment. Or was it just that the difficult demands of day by day living at Mount Hermon made everything else fade into the background?

However we may interpret her silence about what she was doing and thinking when away from Mount Hermon, the fact remains that her students had almost no idea of that side of her life. They knew, of course, about her rheumatic attacks and must have heard about her trips to the sanitarium at Battle Creek, Michigan, and to the baths at Hot Springs, Arkansas, for on these journeys Sarah Dickey had taken a Mount Hermon woman to help her as a practical nurse. On their return the nurses would have had much to tell. Also, Mr. Claude Inge spoke of a letter she wrote from Hot Springs asking him to send her a hundred dollars.

But that Sarah Dickey once journeyed as far as California, no one seems to have known. Indeed, had it not been for a letter from her preserved in the Mount Holyoke alumnae archives, the fact would have been lost. Yet the letter shows how much the experience meant to her. It is dated April 19, 1900 and was written to the former Mount Holyoke Seminary teacher spoken of earlier, Miss Anna C. Edwards, who at the time was visiting Mrs. Mills at Mills College in Oakland, California. In the course of the letter Sarah Dickey wrote,

I was in that beautiful land of sunshine and flowers once, so I know where you are. Hope dear Mrs. Mills is enjoying good health and still enjoying her lovely school. I wonder if dear Mr. and Mrs. Cogswell of Oakland are still living. If I knew their address I should write to them. They so kindly entertained my friend and myself a whole month seven or eight years ago.

Later in this same letter after expressing regret that Miss Edwards was not feeling well, she writes, "But it seems to me you could not find a more desirable place in the world for health, comfort and happiness." There is no clue as to why she went to California or with what friend, but at least we know from this letter the approximate date — 1892 or '93. Mrs. Mills was a prominent Mount Holyoke alumna, class of 1845, who with her husband, the Rev. Cyrus Mills, founded Mills College, the "lovely school" to which the letter refers and of which, after her husband's death, Mrs. Mills was for many years president.

Another interest in Sarah Dickey's life about which her students seem to have had no idea, although next to Mount Hermon it became her greatest interest, was her relationship to her church, the Church of the United Brethren in Christ, later known as the Evangelical United Brethren Church. Its very name was unfamiliar to the former students questioned. In an earlier chapter the statement is made that Sarah Dickey did not proselytize for her denomination. That is true as far as her own activities went. But it is also true that she wanted her church to establish a mission in Clinton.

In the difficult first five years of the Seminary she had already broached the subject. She had written the missionary society of her church — its official, seldom-used name was the Home, Frontier and Foreign Missionary Society — that there was in Clinton "a favorable opening for the establishment of a mission." In 1879 she had asked the Executive Committee of the missionary society to send a member to investigate, a request refused as "not expedient" at the time. This was just after the dreadful epidemic when her church had done so much to help. Two years later, however, when the invitation was urgently repeated, the recording secretary of the Missionary Board, D. K. Flickenger, was commissioned to go. The urgency of the request had to do with six recent conversions in the Seminary resulting from a so-called protracted meeting. It sounds quite in the Mount Holyoke tradition of Sarah Dickey's day. A minute of the Board reads:

On motion of W. J. Shuey, the Cor. Sec. was instructed to go to Clinton as soon as consistent with other duties for the purpose of forming a class and to receive into the church such persons as in his judgment may be fit for membership and to make such other arrangements with Miss Dickey as they in their judgment may think best.

But when the emissary returned, it was to report that he had not taken the steps mentioned because he did not think "it would be wise to organize a United Brethren Class at Clinton, Miss. at this time as it might antagonize the patrons of Mount Hermon Seminary against Miss Dickey and the good work she is doing." He must have tapped some different sources of information from those Sarah Dickey had access to, for her urgent call carried no hint of difficulty. Nor later in the same year after W. J. Shuey's visit of three days at the Seminary did his long and enthusiastic account throw any light on the decision of the Board to give up the idea of a mission at Clinton. Yet at the same Board meeting a possibly related request from Sarah Dickey was granted. It was "that A. Perkins be received into the first or third church of Dayton, O." Was A. Perkins one of the six converts, we wonder? It is a teasing item that stands alone. Best to retreat to the known fact that there was no further discussion of a mission at Clinton.

It was also during the eighties that Sarah Dickey had correspondence with the Woman's Missionary Association of her church (usually referred to as the W.M.A.) about another of her ideas. Her suggestion was that at Mount Hermon pupils might be trained for missionary work in Africa, the work she had so much wanted to do. We know of the proposal chiefly through an article Mrs. L. K. Miller wrote for the August 1886 number of *Woman's Evangel*. Mrs. Miller at the time was national vice-president of the W.M.A. and later its president. Later still she became a trustee of Mount Hermon. In the course of her article on "The Future of the Colored Race," she threw out this suggestion in her somewhat tortured prose:

May it not be that the W.M.A. can soon reach out a helpful hand to Miss Dickey, who is educating girls for teachers, who, by and by, may go from their warm climate to that of Africa without the peril the white race must undergo? May we not find here forces to Christianize Africa?

Though this particular helpful hand was never held out, Sarah Dickey was able some five years later to interest another organization in her idea. The organization was the Christian and Missionary Alliance of which Rev. A. B. Simpson was president and Miss S. A. Lindenberger his assistant. He became much interested in Sarah Dickey's school and in her idea for a missionary training school. That their plans had matured we know from the following statement at the end of the Mount Hermon catalogue for 1892-'93:

> We hope in the near future to open in connection with this a Missionary Training College under the auspices of the Christian Alliance, of which Rev. A. B. Simpson of New York City is president.

And in the same catalogue in the list of trustees appear the names of Rev. A. B. Simpson and Miss Lindenberger, both of New York City. They are the first non-Mississippian trustees and Miss Lindenberger, the first woman on the Board other than Miss Dickey. Their willingness to serve as trustees as well as the notice in the catalogue would indicate that the plan of a missionary training school at Mount Hermon was well advanced. But for reasons unknown the school never materialized and the names of the two New York trustees soon disappeared from the catalogue. The only further reference is a line in Sarah Dickey's will in which she directs that the two hundred dollars borrowed of Rev. A. B. Simpson be paid him.

This project of the training college had followed Sarah Dickey's unsuccessful attempts, described in the previous chapter, to get either the United Brethren or the A.M.A. to take over Mount Hermon. The California trip falls into this same general period of the early nineties and immediately precedes the years of her closest relationship to her church.

That the memory of such abortive attempts should fade is not strange, but surprising and difficult to understand is the fact that not oné of Sarah Dickey's students with whom I talked, seems to have known anything about her study for and final attainment in 1893 of a license from the Church of the United Brethren to preach the gospel or of her later ordination in that church. She became the Rev. Miss Dickey, a title she apparently did not use in Clinton, though it was used when she was in Ohio. The examination that she took for her license was exacting. A formidable list of books to study is given in the 1889 Church Discipline, the one she would have used. It includes studies of the Bible and Bible history, a primer of Christian Evidence, theological treatises, church history, homiletics and much else. With her vigorous mind and her background of teaching Bible studies at Mount Hermon she must have enjoyed the work.

At the 84th Annual Session of the Miami Conference of the Church of the United Brethren Sarah Dickey and three men were examined individually by a committee, the chairman of which was no other than her old friend, Rev. W. J. Shuey. Though the Discipline recommended written examinations, those the four candidates took were oral. The committee report reads in part, "The examination of each member was creditable, and we recommend that each receive license to preach the gospel." The report was adopted by the Conference and Sarah Dickey became a recognized minister. As a licentiate she also became a member of the Conference, but unless under appointment she could not administer the sacraments. Perhaps it was this restriction that led to her next step. At the Miami Annual Conference of 1894, Rev. Mr. Shuey read a letter from her in which she requested the further step of ordination. The Conference minute reads:

Whereas, Sarah A. Dickey is unable to be present, and in view of her work among the colored people in the South, and the importance of her possessing full powers to perform all the functions of a minister of the gospel, therefore,

Resolved, That we hereby instruct and empower any of our bishops to ordain Sister Dickey by laying on of hands at such time and place during the year as may suit the convenience of the parties interested.

The curator of the church archives writes, "This is an unusual conference action and most interesting. It indicates the high respect the Conference held of Miss Dickey and her work."

Actually Sarah Dickey did not take advantage of this special privilege; possibly there was no available bishop within reach. But in 1896 she was able to attend the Conference again and was ordained by Bishop J. W. Hott, D.D., LL.D., assisted in the solemn service by two presiding elders.

From this time on she administered the Lord's Supper in a communion service at Mount Hermon held the first of each month for the boarding pupils. No one, however, could recall any baptism, marriage or funeral at which she officiated, and she continued to have Negro preachers conduct the Sunday afternoon service. Her own relationship with her church grew more close with the years; she attended the Miami Conference again in 1897 and in 1899, and a letter from her was read at the 1900 session. Yet none of her former students, even those close to her, was familiar with the name of the denomination. They did not think of Sarah Dickey in connection with any particular church. She was a Christian, the best Christian they knew.

In the nineties, Sarah Dickey's last full decade, much happened, as we have seen, both in her personal life and in that of the Seminary. In many ways, in spite of increasing financial difficulties, these were peak years. Mount Hermon had become known and valued throughout the state and beyond it. White people, too, recognized the kind of training received and Mount Hermon students were in demand. The white official in Jackson whose duty it was to administer the written examinations finally required of Negro applicants for teaching positions said he could always tell Mount Hermon candidates by, among other things, the neatness of their papers, the legibility of their handwriting and the accuracy of their spelling. The writer, too, can testify to the excellence of Mount Hermon training, for she had the good fortune to become a friend of one of the five daughters of a well-to-do family, all of them educated at Mount Hermon, and she can speak for the soundness of the education received by her friend and her friend's sisters.

The general acclaim accorded the Seminary must have pleased Sarah Dickey, though what she cared about far more was the effect of Mount Hermon on the lives of its students. The influence of Sarah Dickey's emphasis on being honest, thorough, clean, orderly, punctual, on trying to live pure Christian lives made itself felt. Many of the teachers who went out from the Seminary went with a sense of mission. Their pupils in turn caught from them something of Sarah Dickey's teaching. In that 1901 letter to her classmates she tells something of the school and then says:

And we are very proud of the reports we hear of the grand work our girls are doing throughout this and other states, not only for the development of the intellectual powers, but especially for the improvement of the moral and religious lives of their people. Your hearts would rejoice, as mine does, if you could look into some of the lovely homes and well ordered families of many of our dear Christian girls.

The accounts that came back to her and the homes she visited filled her with real joy. She wrote in a letter two years before her death, comparing Mount Hermon to other schools,

In proportion to the number of workers and the amount of money used, we have turned out as many well-educated and well-trained young women as any other school in the state.

Later in the same letter she characteristically adds,

I do not boast. Many a one in my place would have accomplished much more, but I am so thankful my Heavenly Father has honored me with a little work to do, as best I can, in His vineyard.

In those last full years when she was making such valiant efforts to get the needed endowment as well as raising money to meet the running expenses of maintenance and salaries, we find her becoming, for the first time in her life, introspective and, for the second time, retrospective. She had been so much involved in the practical details of running the Seminary and of getting and spending the money needed each year for its upkeep and operation that she had not had time to think back over the years except once ten or twelve years earlier when she was interviewed for those articles in *Woman's Voice* and again later when she wrote of her life in the *Dew of Hermon*. Now, however, near the end of her life various influences converged to make her think about herself as she had never done before. For one thing the dawn of a new century made most people pause, if only for a moment, to take stock of themselves. For another, Sarah Dickey was now in her sixties, body-weary and aware of diminishing strength. Her days, she realized, were nearing their end. What of the work God had given her to do?

That she was looking back with wonder and praise we know from the last class letter she wrote for '69's round robin. She says:

I have been, and am now, most profoundly interested in the special Providential leading of my life which I can trace very closely from my earliest recollections. One of the most remarkable instances is this.

She proceeds to describe her dream of wandering in the deep wood, coming to the wall and seeing the great field beyond it; then on the very day that Pemberton surrendered Vicksburg to Grant, July 4, 1863, she had a vision that repeated the dream of the night before. She says, "A voice within my soul whispered the meaning of both the dream and the vision." She was to go through this world alone, and work alone. The great field was where she was to work. She wrote:

I feel that I have passed through the woods and am in reality in the large open field of possibilities. I praise God that the possibilities are never limited by the years that are passed.

A spirit of thankfulness for the past and trust in the future pervades this letter.

It is good to know that, though she saw so much still to be done and felt so keenly the need for substantial endowment, she never lost her belief in the future of Mount Hermon Seminary. During the two years between the writing of that letter and her death she had evidently been successful, as she thought, in securing the prospect of considerable aid. In her will, witnessed only two days before her death, she says, "I hope that should my plans mature on or by the first of July next as arranged for, to have the Seminary property entirely unencumbered." We can only guess at these "plans." Perhaps they had to do with the bequest of Miss Belle Eakers, who had been a generous contributor, a bequest that was later to determine the future of the Seminary. But whether it was this bequest or something else, Sarah Dickey, as she lay on what she knew was her deathbed, looked forward with confidence to a richly useful future for Mount Hermon Seminary.

This confidence was the more remarkable when we learn what her executor found out after her death, that there were various mortgages on the property, that teachers' salaries were overdue and that food for the stock was running low. Indeed on the morning after her funeral he told the trustees that there was only one bale of hay left and only enough for one more day of other food for the stock. The fact that she had not been troubled by the situation suggests that there may have been nothing unusual about it. For almost thirty years she had managed the Seminary and managed it well on faith and hard work. Mount Hermon was the Lord's and He had never failed it, though, as she once wryly admitted, He sometimes took a long time coming to its aid. On the other hand her confidence in the future may have come from her knowledge of the plans she expected to mature in July.

It will be remembered that when Claude Inge went to say goodbye to her, he found her not in bed where she was supposd to be but up and about, supervising some workmen. She would go back to her sickbed as soon as the work was finished. This was at the end of December, just thirty-one years from that December day in 1872 on which she had heard those fateful words, "Now is the time to begin your life work."

May not the voice on which she always depended have whispered to her that now was the time to lay down that work? However the truth came to her, she knew. By the middle of January her illness developed into acute pneumonia. In those pre-antibiotic days pneumonia more often than not proved fatal. Sarah Dickey, always unsparing of herself, had little strength left with which to withstand the disease. She asked that her niece, Olive Mather Saum with her husband, be sent for, and later that a message go also to Mary Caldwell Coats, but that message somehow miscarried and, to Mrs. Coats's sorrow, arrived too late.

Accepting what she believed was God's will for her, Sarah Dickey next gave her undivided attention to the matter of her will. She finished it, and on January 21, 1904, her signature was witnessed by Judge Cabiness, who had served as trustee from the beginning, and by two of her teachers, Elizabeth Bletcher and Ruth Fox. The document reflects her life and interests. The Seminary comes first:

I desire the perpetuation of Mount Hermon Seminary as an institution of learning for the education of the young women of the State as it has heretofore been conducted.

Then comes the sentence about her nephew's debt, already quoted, and after that a request that
The trustees employ some good woman or women to carry on the school as I have tried to do for the glory of God and the good of my fellows.

With the Seminary real estate is to go the furniture belonging to the establishment, the pianos and some books and souvenirs given me by my father, all which are known by my neices [sic]. All the supplies and provisions in and belonging to the Seminary are to be used for the continuance of the school until the trustee can make further provisions for that purpose.

Next she takes up her land holdings. Two properties in Dickeyville had evidently not been paid for; they are bequeathed to the Seminary. One of them, however, the John Martin house and lot, is given with the request "that said John Martin be allowed to occupy it as a home as long as he keeps it in repair and pays the taxes on the same." She further asks that after his death the place be used for similar "benevolent purposes." The trustees of the Seminary are directed to collect and turn over to the Seminary any monies due on the Dickeyville properties or for the sale of further lots.

The rest of the will concerns bequests except for the payment of the $200 that she owed the Christian and Missionary Alliance. Her first bequest was to her nephew, Charles Surface,

$1,000 and the already mentioned cancellation of the debt he owed her. Another $1,000 bequest was to her niece, Olive Mather Saum and also half of a farm in another county that had been given in lieu of some school fees. The other half of the farm was to go to her other niece, Maud Mather. Then out of any monies or properties remaining she would like to give $100.00 each to two missionary boards of the United Brethren Church. Limited as were her means, she had always contributed to her church. The next item contained bequests to the teachers who were "here now," as she expressed it, $50.00 each to Miss Bletcher, Miss Irvine, Miss Fox, and Miss Simison; $100.00 to her aunt, Miss Adaline Taylor, and finally, $25.00 each to two of the young people she had brought up from childhood, Claude Inge and Willette Campbell Davis. Her nephew-in-law, Claude Saum, was named executor.

The will completed to her satisfaction, Sarah Dickey lay back in peace. Her work in this world was done. Two days later, on Saturday, January 23, 1904, as her friends watched by her bedside, she opened her eyes, smiled, and whispered, "All is well. All is done. Goodbye! Let the work go on as usual." Then she closed her eyes and within an hour she was gone.

The funeral two days later was, to quote a local newspaper account, "attended by a large crowd of colored people and a number of white friends, among them several professors and students from Mississippi College." The Rev. Frank J. Woodworth, D.D., president of Tougaloo University, conducted the service. The president of Mississippi College, the Rev. William T. Lowry, also spoke, paying what was described as "a beautiful tribute to Miss Dickey's character and work." There is no record of President Woodworth's words, but in an article he wrote a year later for the *Mount Holyoke Monthly* he reports President Lowry as having said that the two things the South needed were that all white people should be as pure, upright, loving and unselfish as Miss Dickey and that all colored people should become as pure, upright, loving and unselfish as Miss Dickey tried to have them become. President Woodworth began his article with this sentence: "Among the heroic figures called into prominence by the freeing of the slaves was Sarah A. Dickey." Under the title "A Noble Life," a long unsigned account of Sarah Dickey appeared in the *Tougaloo News,* dated February, 1904, less than a month after her death. She had evidently made a deep impression on the neighboring institution.

After the funeral service in the chapel at Mount Hermon, Sarah Dickey's body was buried on the campus in the spot she had chosen where the Inge girls, Mrs. Coats's baby and Granny Sukey-Bukey already lay, a lovely spot in a grove of pine. Was it her memory of Mary Lyon's grave on the Mount Holyoke campus that had led her to this choice of resting place? The Rev. C. P. Jones, a colored minister from Jackson, conducted the service at the grave. No member of her own church was present.

Later a dignified granite tombstone was erected to mark the spot. The name, Sarah A. Dickey, is cut in a semicircle at the top, the initial "A" forming the keystone of the arc, and below it the following four lines:

> Founder and Principal
> of Mt. Hermon Seminary
> Born Apr. 25, 1838.
> Died Jan. 23, 1904.

Still later, some fifty years later, when all vestiges of the school were gone and the tombstone stood in an uncared-for tangle of bush and trees, the Mississippi State Federation of Colored Women's Clubs put an ornamental metal fence around the grave and planted two yews by it. A memorial service with speeches, hymns and the laying of a wreath at the foot of the tombstone, marked the dedication of their gift.

The morning after the funeral a two-column article appeared on the front page of the *Clarion Ledger,* a leading Jackson daily paper. It carried the following headlines:

> Miss Sarah Dickey Dead
> Principal of a Negro School near Clinton
> She Had Labored under Many Difficulties but
> Overcame Them All

The article that followed told something of her life and the development of Mount Hermon. We read that

She was a woman of strong character, devoted to her work among the blacks and did not seem to care if she was socially ostracised. She maintained that she had been commanded by God to come South and labor in the field that she occupied, and no power on earth could have changed her.

Toward the end we are told that

She had a hard time for several years, but in due course of time the fame of her school went abroad, and pupils came from every direction. The result was that she prospered and died owner of a handsome property and one of the best private negro schools in the state.

On the day after the funeral the trustees of Mount Hermon Seminary met to consider how they might carry out Sarah Dickey's dying request that the school go on "as usual." Mr. Claude Saum as executor of the will met with them and made the state of affairs all too clear. Sobering as the news was, they decided to continue "for the present" in the hope that something more permanent might be worked out for the future. Mrs. Saum, who before her recent marriage had been associate principal in her aunt's school, agreed to act as principal for the three-and-a-half remaining months of the school year. Rev. George Whitfield, president of the Board of Trustees, with Dr. Provine, a professor of chemistry at Mississippi College, took over the work of collecting notes due the Seminary. In short, each was assigned or assigned himself some special task. The Hon. W. E. Mollison from Vicksburg, as this Negro trustee was designated in the catalogue, agreed to send out an appeal to the Negroes in Mississippi for immediate help.

A Clinton newspaper reported this meeting in the rich rhetoric of the day.

The trustees of Mt. Hermon Seminary met yesterday in the rooms which the noble and self-sacrificing Sarah A. Dickey had hallowed and with her dying request before them decided to continue the work which she had carried on at such pains, and under such discouragements. She came in the wake of the war and by her gentleness and devotion bound up wounds and scattered an almost holy light from that moment until her sacred clay rested in the bosom of Mississippi, the adopted state which she had loved so long and served so faithfully.

Miss Dickey had enlisted among her friends some of the best men in the community. The President of trustees is the venerable and scholarly Rev. George Whitfield whose good influence has been impressed upon the lives of thousands who are now leaders of thought in the community, Judge Cabiness, a leading citizen, secretary, and Dr. C. H. Brough, a leading educator. The above are white.

The article goes on to list more curtly the colored trustees. Then it takes up the financial condition of the school, tells of the arrangements made for the rest of the year and speaks of the uncertainty of the future.

That there was great uncertainty about the future of Mount Hermon Seminary no one could deny. Heretofore the role of the trustees had been largely consultative and advisory. Their names in the annual catalogue lent prestige to the Seminary and their advice was useful, but Sarah Dickey did all the real work. Now they were faced with a different situation. They could and would get through the present school year. But what of the future?

9. Aftermath

THE FUTURE lay in the hands of Mount Hermon's trustees, eight of them Mississippians, four white and four colored. The biracial pattern Sarah Dickey established in the seventies had held through the years. The remaining two, both from Dayton, Ohio, had taken the place of the two from New York City who had served so briefly. The Ohio names are familiar to us — Dr. W. J. Shuey (he had evidently acquired a D.D. somewhere along the way), friend to Sarah Dickey for more than twenty years and prominent churchman, and Mrs. L. K. Miller, active in the missionary work of the United Brethren. All ten felt bound by the deathbed request that the school go on "as usual," bound also by the obvious community need for a school. Yet they knew they had neither the means nor the know-how to manage such an institution.

Their only hope was to find some organization interested in educational work for Negroes and willing to adopt Mount Hermon. That they thought at once of the American Mission-ary Association was natural, even though they remembered its refusal of Mount Hermon fourteen years earlier. The A.M.A. had schools all over the South and much can change in fourteen years. They may not have known that by 1904 the A.M.A. was more interested in getting the rural South to recognize and shoulder its responsibilty for Negro elementary education than in taking on more schools. Its policy was to turn over its ele-mentary schools to local authorities as soon as local conditions warranted the action and concentrate on its more advanced schools and colleges. Therefore it was not interested in adding to its holdings, especially a school burdened with debt and in

153

the same county as their own Tougaloo. Not interested, that is, until Dr. Shuey came forward with a proposal that caused the Board to reconsider.

He had been entrusted with the disposal of a ten thousand dollar legacy left by Miss Mary Belle Eakers of Dayton, Ohio, "for the benefit and education of Freedmen in the South." If Sarah Dickey had lived the money would probably have gone to Mount Hermon, for Miss Eakers had been a regular and generous donor to it. But since the sum was not large enough to provide permanence for the Seminary, Dr. Shuey offered it to the A.M.A. on the understanding that the Association take over and operate Mount Hermon as long as there should be a need for the school. The Association, always in want of ready money for its work in the South, agreed and the much relieved trustees bowed themselves out, feeling they had saved Mount Hermon. Also, as Dr. Shuey somewhat grandiloquently put it, "the gift of a godly woman would be placed where it would bless the negro for all time."

In the next Mount Hermon catalogue, that for 1904-05, this statement appears:

. . . the Seminary has passed into the hands of the American Missionary Association, the Society which, since 1846, has been engaged in planting churches, schools and missions among the needy millions in our own country. . . . With such an Association to direct and watch over its interests, Mount Hermon Seminary should continue to follow the high religious, intellectual and industrial aims set before it in the early days of its founder.

Also to be noticed in this catalogue is the omission of the Advanced Course, the course that Sarah Dickey had expected to become in time the main course of the Seminary. She had scrupulously reserved the Mount Hermon diploma for graduation from it.

The agreement arrived at for Mount Hermon's future seemed to all concerned highly satisfactory. Actually it was anything but that. It sounded Mount Hermon's death knell, though the dying school lingered on for twenty years. Looking back, we see that it could hardly have been otherwise, for this stepchild of the Association was in the same general locality as Tougaloo, its own child. Sooner or later economy would suggest to its absentee owners in New York that the Normal Course and perhaps boarding pupils as well might profitably be transferred to the larger institution, thus reducing Mount Hermon to an elementary school which in time could be dropped. And that is what, little by little, came to pass.

Hindsight makes us wish that the two trustees from Sarah Dickey's church in Dayton had tried to persuade their church to take Mount Hermon under its wing. Individual members of that church had given generously to Mount Hermon, and Sarah Dickey's yearly visits to Dayton had kept it in close touch with the work. Had the Church of the United Brethren taken over the Seminary and had the right personnel been found, Mount Hermon might today be the realization of its founder's dream and the name of Sarah Dickey be as well known as that of Mary Lyon.

The right personnel — perhaps that might have saved the school in spite of its proximity to Tougaloo and its absentee ownership. The first principal appointed, Miss Lillie Bletcher, seemed an excellent choice, for she had been associate principal after Olive Mather's marriage and knew the work and Sarah Dickey's ideals. But she stayed only one year, 1904-05. Next the Association sent as principal someone previously unconnected with the school, Miss Julia Elwin of Merrimacport, Massachusetts. During the four years of her principalship the staff continued to number five, but on her departure it was cut to three. Miss Ruth Simison, who had come to Mount Hermon in the fall before Sarah Dickey's death, was named principal. This drastic reduction had nothing to do with the number of pupils, which veered erratically from year to year, up and down, down and up. It ranged from 59 to 110, the boarding department from 10 to 45. In a letter to one of Sarah Dickey's classmates Miss Simison describes the situation and, without knowing it, something of her own inadequacy. She acknowledges a "generous gift to our school" and then tells of the struggle to keep Mount Hermon going. She writes,

. . . but since I became principal three years ago, it has been a greater struggle since our faculty has been cut down to three, a colored matron who teaches cooking, Miss Fox who was with her [Miss Dickey] three years before I came, and myself, the entire grade work devolving on us two.

We are almost in despair this year, for our need of another teacher who can assist in the grades and in preparing for our special exercises especially those at commencement, is desperate. For two years we have had advanced pupils who were taking normal training under Miss Fox and were able to do this, but they are gone, and it seems we must have help from some quarter to save the reputation of the school, not to say anything of our school efficiency. The community expects grand closing exercises — as usual, but with four grades each (besides numerous divisions in the lower grades) and my pressing duties outside the school-room as principal, superintendent of the farm, home, and school, it is superhuman to be able to carry it through and carry on the regular school work.

Yet for the next seven years the two carried on, doing their inadequate best to follow in Sarah Dickey's footsteps. They were earnest, devout women who made a place for themselves in the Negro community, but they lacked the training, imagination and initiative necessary for the work they were trying to do. Loyal to the memory of Sarah Dickey, they celebrated the anniversary of her death as a Founders Day. A few of Sarah Dickey's classmates visited the school and continued to take an interest in it. We read in the 1911-'12 catalogue about a gift from one of them: "Through the generosity of Miss Martha Hathaway of Claremont, Cal., a cookery department has been opened." But well-wishers could do little in the face of the Association's indifference. The property, so carefully cared for by Sarah Dickey, drifted into disrepair.

That Mount Hermon still commanded respect in spite of the slow erosion of such indifference is shown by the report of a federal government survey of Negro education in private schools made in 1914 and rechecked in 1916. The report recommended that Mount Hermon turn over its elementary work to the public schools and devote itself to training teachers for rural schools. The Mount Hermon trained teachers still in the field had made a name for the Seminary. The A.M.A., however, paid no attention to this recommendation, its indifference largely a matter of policy. Its point of view was reasonable enough, for by concentrating all teacher training at nearby Tougaloo, economy was effected. As for turning over the elementary work to the public schools, that the A.M.A. intended to do as soon as local conditions warranted the change. Perhaps because they saw the desired end in view and wanted to make the last years easier for the two harassed and overburdened teachers, they provided a third teacher for the last four years.

In this whole matter the Association acted in good faith. As absentee owner it shared the disability common to absentee ownership. People on the spot know things hidden or not understood by those at a distance. For instance, the Association had no understanding of the passionate devotion of the Negro community to Miss Dickey's school, "Dickeystute," as it was affectionately called, placing it with and distinguishing it from the popular Central Female Institute made famous by Walter Hillman and generally referred to as the "Stute." The part Mount Hermon had played in the Negro communal life was not considered or perhaps not known by the Northern officials. They thought only in terms of the white community and its obligation to take care of the elementary education of its Negro children. Those at Mount Hermon knew little if anything of the Association's intentions. After the retirement of Dr. Woodworth, Sarah Dickey's friend, Tougaloo and Mount Hermon saw little of one another. The new Tougaloo president, Rev. William F. Holmes, well briefed on the Association's plans for Mount Hermon, saw no reason for taking an interest in it. There was only casual visiting back and forth. The fifteen mile buggy ride on the back roads that connected the two institutions was a pleasant one, and the lovely old Calvert house even in its run-down condition an attraction. Tougaloo teachers on their return from an outing at Mount Hermon told tales of chickens walking in and out of the once carefully kept halls. Perhaps they laughed among themselves when Miss Simison and Miss Fox visited Tougaloo, for they came not for the purpose of visiting classes and picking up new ideas but to emphasize Miss Dickey's dying request that Mount Hermon go on "as usual."

It was as though they felt some breath of change in the air and wanted to make clear their obedience to that request. They proudly explained that they were using the very same texts Miss Dickey had used twenty years earlier. They little realized the part their own inadequacies played in what was impending — the end of Sarah Dickey's dream.

Final action came when the American Missionary Association received the full account requested of conditions at Mount Hermon. It was written by Tougaloo's dean, Dean Cobb, who with his wife had been sent by President Holmes to investigate. The action is recorded in the Association's report for 1924:

> Mt. Hermon Seminary, Clinton, Miss. has been under observation for a number of years with reference to its permanent need in the community. Its property is in a sad condition and something radical needs to be done. With Tougaloo only a dozen miles distant there was no thought of expanding the work and particularly because the local community should be made responsible for providing free elementary education, it was voted in April that Mt. Hermon be closed the last of May. Proceeds from the sale of the property will be used in erecting a girls' dormitory at Tougaloo in memory of Miss Sarah Dickey, founder of the school. This is in accordance with the agreement made by the Association with Mt. Hermon's trustees nineteen years ago. Unfortunately the property is of little value and practically unsalable.

The Negro community in and around Clinton knew nothing of this decision until President Holmes made the announcement at Mount Hermon's commencement, May 1924. That commencement! More than one person has tried to describe to the writer the effect of President Holmes' ultimatum. A bomb exploding in their midst could not have been more shattering. Stupefaction was followed by disbelief. This was their school, center of their communal life! Their Miss Dickey had made it for them. Though it had been twenty years since her death, she was still a living presence among them.

Something of all this must have reached official ears, for in the October issue of *The American Missionary*, organ of the Association, there is an article entitled "The Passing of an Institution" that is very different in tone from that of the report quoted above. It begins,

An institution like a person develops a personality. The decease of a worthy institution is also accompanied by sorrow and regret as is the decease of a noble individual. This is particularly and peculiarly true of Mount Hermon Seminary, Clinton, Mississippi. Miss Sarah Dickey was an unusual individual. She lived by faith. She was led as the historic mystics were led — not so much by reason and sight, as by faith and insight. Singlehanded she undertook to secure an education at Mount Holyoke. Alone and unafraid, she dared a half century ago to do for Negro children what the love of God and Mount Holyoke had done for her.

The article goes on to speak of Mount Hermon, of the Association's connection with it, of the decision to give up the school and ends with the following:

It is hoped that this action will stimulate the community's sense of responsibility and that within a few years the free elementary schools will increase in number and improve in method and leadership, inspiring many of its pupils to continue their education at Tougaloo. When this is done the many sacrifices of Miss Dickey and her faithful successors will have been vindicated.

Vindication, if vindication is necessary, did not have to wait for the future. As far as Sarah Dickey was concerned, it was in the hands of those who had known and loved her, the local Negroes. Perhaps what they did at this juncture shows more clearly than anything else her influence. It was not just that so long after her death they wanted to preserve something of what she had done, but even more, that they had the confidence and courage to act. Negroes of that time were generally inexperienced in group action and lacking in initiative. Yet these Negroes decided that if Mount Hermon was to be sold, they would buy it. Even though they could not continue the school, the property should belong to their people and serve their needs as in the days of Miss Dickey. A self-appointed group of ten men took charge. Thirty years later, though some had died and others had moved away, I had no difficulty in learning the names of all but one of the group. They deserve to be recorded: Lawrence Anthony, Parker G. Cooper, Claude Inge, Rev. Paul Johnson, Robert Johnson, Aaron Putnam, Allen Putnam, C. C. Sims, and Coleman Wilkerson.

When the ten men heard that the property was held at $7,500, of which amount $2,000 must be in cash, they wrote to President Holmes, the Association's agent for the property, asking for the refusal of it. They had already begun collecting the money when his reply came. It set them back on their heels. He wrote that he would not sell it to them under any circumstances, and he changed the terms to cash payment of the entire amount. Not having his side of the story we find it difficult to understand this seemingly arbitrary action. But those who were at Touglaoo then and knew President Holmes think that he acted with the interest of Negro education at heart. They said that he probably felt that the men could not raise the money and his change in the terms would be to convince them of the fact. Furthermore, even supposing they could get the money, he would feel, they argued, and they agreed with him, that the school would be continued under the same management and go from bad to worse; whereas if it were closed the responsibility for the education of Clinton Negroes would be placed on the town where it belonged.

When the men recovered from the shock of President Holmes' letter, they refused to regard the matter as closed. They laid their plans and bided their time. It came when, no other offer having been made, the property was put up at auction to sell for not less than $7,500. The auctioneer had arranged with his son-in-law to buy it for him at that price. In the absence of other bidders it was knocked down to the son-in-law. Immediately the Negroes went into action. They secured an injunction to stay the sale until the ten of them could bring suit to test the legality of President Holmes's refusal to sell the property to them.

They also had plans, should they win the suit and get possession of the property, for disposing of it in a way that would ensure its use for their people, a use of which their Sarah Dickey would approve. The Mississippi State Federation of Colored Women's Clubs stood ready to buy the property of them for a much needed project. The Federation, founded in 1906, was and is an important, public spirited, hard working organization.

How many were in it at that time is not remembered; in the early fifties, the total membership of its eighty clubs was over a thousand. The project the Federation had in mind was to establish a training school, or reformatory as it was then called, for delinquent Negro boys. There was a state supported one for white boys, but none for Negroes. Mount Hermon with its dormitories, school rooms, chapel and farm offered just the facilities they needed for such an undertaking.

At last the case was decided and, as might be expected, in favor of the A.M.A. Mr. R. S. Wither's purchase of the property stood, but, finding no other buyers, he sold it to the Negroes. What they paid for it, we do not know. But the records of the State Federation of Colored Women's Clubs show that the Federation bought it from the ten men at a "reduced" price of $7,848.26. The property once more belonged to the people for whose benefit Sarah Dickey had purchased it in 1874.

The federated ladies decided to name their school the Margaret Murry Washington Home for Delinquents after Booker T. Washington's Mississippi-born wife. It was launched with an impressive dedication service on April 18, 1930. A long-felt want would be filled when once they got into full operation. At the start, since none of them had had experience in such work, they took only four boys. However, a beginning had been made and general satisfaction prevailed.

But not for long! On November 10, 1930 the four boys, unused to restrictions and irked by them, decided with the ruthless logic of youth that if the building which housed them were to burn down, they could no longer live in it. It did burn down, completely. So did the building to which they were moved, Mrs. Calvert's fine old residence with its five marble mantel pieces where Sarah Dickey had started her school. With the two main buildings gone, it was clear that the club women had undertaken more than they could handle. Three of the boys were sent to Prentiss and the fourth to Piney Woods where Dr. Laurence Jones had already developed his well-regimented and now well-known school.

The Margaret Murry Washington Home for Delinquents was no more. Yet the failure of their own effort did not discourage these concerned women. They continued to work for such a school. At last, in 1942, the State of Mississippi established a Reformatory for Delinquent Negro Juveniles and in its biennial report to the Legislature we read the following generous admission:

Among those who worked for the establishment of this institution over a long period of time was the Mississippi State Federation of Colored Women's Clubs. These women contacted white leaders — governors and legislators — until finally their efforts were successful.

The Federation was also busy finding other uses for their property that would benefit their race. They gave ten acres to Hinds County for Negro school sites. A much needed county high school was dedicated in 1956. They leased, for a nominal dollar, seventy-five acres for a Scout camp for boys, Camp Labaloo, and later, on the other side of the land, twenty-five acres for Camp Minnehaha, the Scout camp for girls. This last was made less desirable in 1961-62 by the county taking by eminent domain ten acres for a stadium. Though the county paid $7,000 for the land, the women did not want to give it up. It cut their property in two and interfered with the privacy of the girls' camp. Earlier they had built a club house for themselves and erected the ornamental metal fence around Sarah Dickey's grave. (Apparently they did not know of the other burials there.)

The Negro elementary school that had been transferred to the Mount Hermon property from the Sumner Hill locality brought its name with it, and when the high school was built, it, too, took the Sumner Hill name. There are, unfortunately, no names to recall the old days, but on the school grounds there are two reminders of them. One is the bell that had served Mount Hermon and the Negro community so well. When the Seminary was closed and what could be used at Tougaloo, including the bell, was to be moved there, the Negroes had begged that the bell, so full of memories for them, be left in its place, a plea that was granted. We already know about the second reminder on what was once Mount Hermon property, Sarah Dickey's grave, now well cared for by the Federation of Colored Women's Clubs.

Other reminders in the form of memorials are on two college campuses — one far away in a building at Sarah Dickey's alma mater, the other nearby at Tougaloo. The Mount Holyoke one is the gift of Sarah Dickey's classmates; that at Tougaloo is the fulfillment of the agreement made in 1904 when the management of the school was transferred. The class of 1869 at its fiftieth reunion in 1919 (a reunion, incidentally, at which the class had present the largest proportion of living graduates of any reuning class) took up the question of their gift to the College. A year and a half earlier Mount Holyoke had lost by fire one of its main science buildings. It had therefore embarked on a three million dollar money-raising campaign for replacing the science building and for other pressing needs. It was a formidable sum in those days for a woman's college to undertake. All alumnae were alerted. The classes were told that five thousand dollars would equip a laboratory which could be named for anyone the class chose. The class of 1869 welcomed the suggestion. They had no difficulty in deciding that of all the thirty-eight who had graduated so long ago, Sarah Dickey was the one they most wanted to honor. How surprised and puzzled she would have been at their decision! Contributions came in from every living graduate of the class, from some nongraduates, from family and friends of those no longer living. At the end it was recorded in the alumnae office that the class of 1869 had given five thousand dollars for the Dickey memorial and twelve thousand for the general fund. When Clapp Laboratory, the name chosen for the new building, was opened in 1924, a brass plaque was placed in what is now a physiology laboratory. The framed photograph of Sarah Dickey that used to hang near it has gone, but the plaque remains. It reads:

Dickey Laboratory
Gift of the Class of 1869
To honor their classmate
Sarah Dickey

Three years later, in 1927, the second memorial took form on the Tougaloo campus in accordance with the agreement made twenty-three years earlier when Mount Hermon was turned over to the American Missionary Association. By that agreement, as we know, if the property was ever sold, the proceeds should be used for a building at Tougaloo named in memory of Sarah Dickey. The first idea was that the building would be a girls' dormitory. Then a domestic science building seemed an even greater need and being in line with Sarah Dickey's interests, was the second claimant for the name. But a fire that destroyed the old wooden hospital settled the question, need taking precedence over appropriateness. A one-story red brick hospital was built and dedicated on October 25, 1927 as the Sarah A. Dickey Memorial Hospital. Gifts from alumni and interested friends were added to the relatively small amount received from the sale of Mount Hermon. The American Missionary Association provided a twelve thousand dollar endowment. The dedication was a big affair. Officials came down from New York, other friends came from various parts of the country, alumni gathered, and Dr. Provine, President of Mississippi College and long-time friend of Sarah Dickey, came from Clinton to tell about her. A large framed picture of her was propped up on the platform together with her framed Mount Holyoke diploma. These were later hung in the entrance hall of the new building where, I believe, they still are. President Holmes in his opening remarks, according to the account given in the *Tougaloo News,* made statements that showed how little he knew about Mount Hermon. For instance, he said that Sarah Dickey founded a school for colored children which with her advancing years the American Missionary Association took over! His patent ignorance may throw further light on his refusal to sell the property to the Negroes. The larger part of the program had to do with other donors, with the Tougaloo alumni and with the use for which the hospital was intended, the final speaker being the head of the Mississippi State Board of Health. The Sarah A. Dickey Memorial Hospital served its purpose for more than thirty years. Now, at the moment of

writing, the building is being used to house faculty. But its
name has been retained and when the pressure for faculty housing is relieved it will probably be restored to its place as the
college infirmary.

So much for these man-made memorials. Another kind, one
every human being leaves behind, however briefly, is the re-
membrance of him in the minds and hearts of those who have
known him. A name is mentioned and for many of us a picture
of the person flashes before our inner eye followed by a rush
of memories connected with him. Such pictures and such memories the writer tried to elicit from more than twenty former
students of Sarah Dickey whom she was able to locate. They
were women and men in their sixties and seventies, a few even
older, little accustomed to putting their thoughts and feelings
into words, but eager to help anyone interested in their Miss
Dickey. Often the woman who answered the knock at her
cabin door would greet the writer with a sullen look that
seemed to say, "White woman, go away!" But Sarah Dickey's
name was magic. The sullen look gave way to smiles and the
intruder was cordially welcomed. In what they told there is an
absence of eulogy or remarks like that of Sarah Dickey's friend,
Rev. W. J. Shuey, who said that when she left after staying
with his family on her visits to Dayton, they felt as though they
had entertained an angel. Her Negro friends were much more
impressed by her human aspects. Their attempts at description
were full of unangelic detail. "She wasn't coarse, and she
wasn't too fine," one man said, admitting his inability to describe her. "She was just a good common woman." Another,
who had been brought up by her, was more definite. "She was
a handsome woman, stocky, must have weighed 160 pounds,
very clear blue eyes, very active but not bustly." "She walked
soft," yet another remarked. A Normal Course graduate called
her "fine looking, not large, not small, full busted. She wore
grey tailored clothes and was very erect." Several spoke of her
horsemanship. "She drove a span of brown horses, drove like
a man. Was a woman and a man too. Wasn't above doing anything at all." It was a man who spoke particularly of her voice.

"An extra fine voice," he said, "clear and carrying. It seemed to ring. You remembered what she said. She talked a lot about starting right in where you was. Forget past mistakes and bad things. Put all you've got into today and then when it comes into tomorrow." This last was an idea others spoke of, too, starting fresh, forgetting the bad past. "Forgit all that," one of them put it. And another, "You always understood her when she talked. She took time to tell you good. She was patient but firm."

These glimpses of how Sarah Dickey appeared to those among whom she lived and for whom she spent herself help us to see her as the active, vital woman she was, but they do not help us to understand how she was able to do all she did, endure all she had to endure, carry on her school in spite of apparently insurmountable obstacles and remain her cheerful, buoyant self. The early picture of the silent, withdrawn little drudge in her aunt's home offers no promise of the woman she became nor does that of the thin, harassed young woman working her difficult way through Mount Holyoke. Yet the motivating force for all she was and did becomes clear as we examine her life. It comes from her sense of closeness to God, a personal, intimate relationship that sustained her. Communication came in different ways. Her first mention is of an "inner voice." Next she speaks of dreams and visions — the dark woods, the open fields and the wall that was finally removed. But the most frequent means of communication was through a voice. Sometimes the Lord spoke to her directly, sometimes through a messenger as when in her first month at Mount Holyoke she was told what the Lord expected her to do and she cried out, "No, that could not be the voice of God. . . ." Unwilling to admit it, yet subconsciously recognizing it, she was anxious and uneasy until in her last year the matter was settled. It was the one time that her obedience to the voice was not immediate and unquestioning. Though given to using many capital letters, she never capitalized "voice." Perhaps it is part of the natural, normal everydayness of the relationship — no kneeling, no thou-ing, just the outpouring of her heart at the moment. Her characteristic desire to be completely truthful in so important a matter appears in her use of the word "seemed' in many of the accounts. Telling of the direction she received in 1872 to start her school, she writes "suddenly there seemed to come before me a flash of light, and a voice said 'Now is the time to begin your life work.' " After the Clinton riot she takes the Lord into her confidence.

Lord, you see the people are all scattered and away from their homes, and it looks as if we can never get them together or do them any good. . . . O Lord, what am I doing anyway? what am I working for? And a voice spoke in my soul so sweetly and said 'You are working for Christ.' Immediately the burden rolled off my shoulders and I arose and went to work again with a cheerful heart.

A student interested in the psychology of religious experience would find a rich field in Sarah Dickey's life. The traumatic experience of her mother's death, her removal to her aunt's home at a distance where she met with little love and was valued chiefly for the work she could do, made her lean in spirit on a growing sense she had of her mother's gentle presence. Though she came under no religious influence from the time of her mother's death until after her sixteenth year, she tells us that she had always felt a reaching out of her spirit to something above and beyond her. So when she was introduced to the warm fellowship of the United Brethren in Christ first at Lewisburg and later in Dayton, she found what she had been reaching for and recognized the source of that inner voice she had already come to rely on. Her twentieth birthday when she became a church member was an important day in her life, but it marked no sudden conversion like that of Saul of Tarsus, no change in her way of life like that of Francis of Assisi. It was rather the glad arrival at the home toward which, without knowing it, she had been journeying.

But it is not until Mount Hermon had actually opened and the long struggle begun to develop it into a second Mount Holyoke that we see the full flowering of her faith. True, she worked as hard as a human being can work, but she was free from the corroding effect of anxiety. Her complete faith left her spirit quiet and relaxed. Perhaps more than anything else that was what gave her the power to do all she did.

Study of the effect of a person's innermost convictions on that person's life is of perennial interest to most of us. Of more immediate and local interest is a look at Sarah Dickey's life as a case history in race relations. She settled in Clinton during the Reconstruction period when anti-North and anti-Negro feelings were at their height. She could not have arrived at a worse time nor could she have done anything worse than to room and board in the home of a Negro. She was consequently treated by the white citizens like an outcast, shunned like a leper. Yet in less than twenty years she could write her class-mates that all prejudice against her was gone — "completely."

How did such a change come about? Much as she longed to be accepted, she had made no direct assault on prejudice and no direct attempt at reconciliation. She had simply gone on her way doing what she had come to do. God had given her a special task. He had not given her the right to judge those who had made that task necessary. His ways were past finding out. But she knew these persecutors were His children too. Her part was to accept them all, black and white, as her brothers and sisters. The Negro who said that Sarah Dickey did not know any difference between white and colored spoke the truth. Yet there was a difference in that the Negroes needed her help because of what the long years of their servitude had done to them. She remembered the difficulties Moses encountered in leading the children of Israel, weakened as they, too, were by their years of servitude. Not that she thought of herself as a Moses. She was far too humble-minded for that. But it en-couraged her to remember what splendid, independent people the children of Israel finally became and how loyal to their God. She saw what the colored people in Clinton needed and to the best of her ability she supplied that need. The whole town benefited by what she did, and in consequence race rela-tions improved.

Another thing to observe in Sarah Dickey's handling of race relations is that she always acted directly wherever she could by bringing white and Negro together on equal terms. Witness her biracial Board of Trustees. No tokenism there — half white and half colored, with its first president a Negro and all its members men who carried weight among their fellows. For the men on the Board, both white and colored, the association was a liberalizing experience. We notice with interest the absence of any mention of race in the name of the Seminary or in any of the catalogues published during Sarah Dickey's lifetime. Nor is anything made of the presence of white students in the school — her niece, the children of white staff members, *et al.* (This was before there was a state school segregation law.) Such integration as there was did not spring from any theory; it was just the natural result of circumstances and taken for granted. Sarah Dickey did not make issues out of her actions. Consequently she did not arouse antagonism.

To be sure, things might have been different if after the cold-blooded political murder of Charles Caldwell, Walter Hillman had not joined her Board of Trustees and stepped into Caldwell's place as president of it. Though a Northerner, he and his wife, as we know, had built themselves into the life of their adopted state before the war. The presence of a man of Walter Hillman's caliber and standing in the community made a difference. Elected president of the Mississippi State Teachers' Association, he used his position to plead for more and better common school education for *all*. After saying in one of his speeches:

In vain are armies and navies and fortifications for the preservation of its liberties to a free people, unless good morals and general intelligence are its possession

he goes on to say that the law of self-preservation demands common schools for all and that the greatness of a state depends on the general system of public instruction. He does not mention Negroes as such. He leaves his audience to make application.

Other supporters of Sarah Dickey came from Mississippi College, the Baptist institution that had first brought Walter Hillman to Clinton and that he rescued and built up after the

war before returning to his own school. There were usually
two from that college on Mount Hermon's Board of Trustees.
Dr. Hillman was succeeded as president of the Board by Rev.
George Whitfield, president of Mississippi College. Another
Mississippi College president, Rev. William T. Lowry, spoke
at Sarah Dickey's funeral. In the climate that such continuing
leadership fostered, racial tension was naturally reduced. During the last ten or fifteen years of Sarah Dickey's life, Clinton,
town of the terrible Clinton riot, basked in the sun of friendly
race relations.

How cheering it is to know that the change here recorded
took place in the heart of Mississippi! Cheering also that this
beneficent change centered in the life and work of a woman
who accepted without reservation the statement that faith can
remove mountains. That the mountain-movers raised up for
her were fellow townsmen is perhaps the most cheering aspect
of this case history, for what has happened once can surely
happen again. Sarah Dickey has blazed the trail. There are
men of good will all through the South to follow it. The power
of an individual must never be underestimated. The life of
Sarah Dickey proves it.

Index

Addenda

Two READERS of the first edition of this book have come forward with material that fills two of the gaps in Sarah Dickey's story. The author hopes that any others who have special knowledge will be equally generous with what they know.

Mrs. Marjorie G. Patterson of Jackson, Mississippi, writes that her great-great-grandfather's youngest brother, Isaac, was Sarah Dickey's father. She has a picture of "Sally" in her family album. The family came of Scottish Covenanter stock. The founder of Sarah Dickey's line, John, was born at sea when his father emigrated to America in colonial days. They probably settled in Pennsylvania along with other Dickeys. Later, John, grown to man's estate, moved South, finally settling in Rowan County, North Carolina, where his son Samuel, Sarah Dickey's grandfather, grew up. Samuel was with Washington at Valley Forge during the Revolutionary War. Returning to North Carolina, he became a warm friend of Daniel Boone. Their friendship led to his going with his family to Kentucky on one of Boone's colonizing trips. Unsettled conditions there made him decide to move again. Family tradition has it that Boone accompanied the Dickey family as far as the Ohio River, where they said goodbye. The Dickeys crossed over to Cincinnati and then pushed up into Butler County, where they settled and where their youngest son, Isaac, Sarah Dickey's father, was born, the first white child born in Madison Township. Orphaned at the age of twelve, Isaac knew little of real home life until his marriage. His wife's maiden name was Tryon.

Mrs. William Hollenbaugh of Middletown, Ohio, has a document dated April 13, 1863 which reads as follows:

Sarah Ann Dickey does hereby agree to teach the school of District No. 2 Madison Township, Butler County, Ohio for the term of three months for $1.00 per day so long as each party is satisfied, school commencing at 8½ o'clock, and adjourning at 4 in the evening. Be careful to shut everything up in the evening and especially on Friday evening.

The contract is signed by the school directors, C. W. Vorhis, Levi Huffman, and G. C. Hetzler, and by Sallie A. Dickey. So now we know that here at the Upper Brown's Run School, as it was locally called, Sarah Dickey held her last teaching position before she left for that momentous experience in Vicksburg.